PENGUIN POPULAR REFERENCE

GREEK PHRASE BOOK

Greek Phrase Book

Nikos Stangos and Jillian Norman

PENGUIN BOOKS

Published by the Penguin Group
Penguin Books Ltd, 27 Wrights Lane, London w8 5TZ, England
Penguin Putnam Inc., 375 Hudson Street, New York, New York 10014, USA
Penguin Books Australia Ltd, Ringwood, Victoria, Australia
Penguin Books Canada Ltd, 10 Alcorn Avenue, Toronto, Ontario, Canada M4V 3B2
Penguin Books (NZ) Ltd, Private Bag 102902, NSMC, Auckland, New Zealand

Penguin Books Ltd, Registered Offices: Harmondsworth, Middlesex, England

First published 1973
10 9 8 7 6 5

Printed in England by Cox & Wyman Ltd, Reading, Berkshire

CONTENTS

Contents

INTRODUCTION

In this series of phrase books only those words and phrases that are essential to the traveller have been included. From a purist point of view, some of the contents of this phrase book would not be 'correct' Greek. But the assumption is that this is a guide for communication with ordinary people in the street and not a method for learning the language in its ideally perfect form. For easy reference the phrases are divided into several sections, each one dealing with a different situation. Some of the Greek phrases are marked with an asterisk – these attempt to give an indication of the kind of reply you may get to your questions, of questions you may be asked, or to indicate street signs and other notices that you should be aware of.

A transcript which incorporates a pronunciation guide is provided for each phrase and each word in the extensive vocabulary list, at the end of the book. In addition there is an explanation of Greek pronunciation at the beginning of the book and a brief survey of the essential points of grammar. It would be advisable to read these sections before starting to use the book.

GREEK PRONUNCIATION

The pronunciation guide is intended for people with no knowledge of modern Greek. As far as possible the system is based on English pronunciation. Each phrase and each word in the vocabulary is transliterated in Roman characters in accordance with this pronunciation guide. As a result complete accuracy may sometimes be lost for the sake of simplicity, but if the reader learns the Greek alphabet and the pronunciation of the letters he should be able to understand modern Greek and make himself understood.

THE ALPHABET

Modern Greek uses the same alphabet as ancient Greek and the spelling of words has remained virtually unchanged. Those who want to use or understand Greek must first learn the alphabet. In spite of the differences between English and Greek this should not be difficult as most of the sounds are relatively easy to make.

The Greek alphabet has twenty-four letters in capitals and lower case.

capital	lower case	
A	α	álpha (as **a** in dart)
B	β	víta (as **v** in van)
Γ	γ	ghámა (as **y** in yellow)
Δ	δ	dhélta (as **th** in this)
E	ε	épsilon (as **e** in let)
Z	ζ	zíta (as **z** in zone)
H	η	íta (as **i** in lit)
Θ	θ	thíta (as **th** in theatre)
I	ι	yióta (as **i** in lit)
K	κ	kápa (as **k** in keep)

Λ	λ	lámda (as **l** in lemon)
Μ	μ	mi (as **m** in man and **i** in lit)
Ν	ν	ni (as **n** in net and **i** in lit)
Ξ	ξ	ksi (as **x** in tax and **i** in lit)
Ο	ο	ómikron (as **o** in pot)
Π	π	pi (as **p** in past and **i** in lit)
Ρ	ρ	ro (as **r** in rain)
Σ	σ, ς[1]	síghma (as **s** in stone)
Τ	τ	taf (as **t** in time)
Υ	υ	ípsilon (as **i** in lit)
Φ	φ	fi (as **f** in fan and **i** in lit)
Χ	χ	hi (as **h** in hat and **i** in lit)
Ψ	ψ	psi (as **ps** in eclipse and **i** in lit)
Ω	ω	omégha (as **o** in pot)

1. Only used at the end of a word.

Vowels

All vowels are pronounced distinctly; unstressed vowels keep their pure sound and are never slurred as in English. The letter e is always pronounced at the end of a word.

(*Note:* Although only lower case will be given from now on, it is assumed that the reader will be able to transfer to capitals once he has familiarized himself with the letters of the alphabet.)

α, ε, η, ι, ο, υ, ω

πανί	pani (cloth)
λέξη	lexi (word)
ρῆμα	rimma (verb)
μάτι	mati (eye)

στόμα   stoma (mouth)
φύλλο   fyllo (leaf)
φῶς   fos (light)

Compound Vowels (Diphthongs)

αι	as e in smell	παιδί	pedhí (child)
ει	as i in lit	είμαι	íme (I am)
οι	as i in lit	όλοι	óli (all)
ου	as oo in cool	πουλί	poolí (bird)
αυ	as af in after	αυτόματος	aftómatos (automatic)
αυ	as av in avarice	αύριο	ávrio (tomorrow)
ευ	as ef in left	ἐλεύθερος	eléftheros (free)
ευ	as ev in seven	νεῦμα	névma (sign)

Consonants

β, γ, δ, ζ, θ, κ, λ, μ, ν, ξ, π, ρ, σ, τ, φ, χ, ψ

βάρκα	várka (boat)
γράμμα	ghrámma (letter)
δέντρο	dhéntro (tree)
ζέστη	zésti (heat)
θέατρο	théatro (theatre)
καλός	kalós (good)
λίγο	lígho (a little)
μάτι	máti (eye)
νερό	neró (water)
ξανά	[1]xaná (again)
πόδι	pódhi (ſʊʊt)
ρῆμα	ríma (verb)
στόμα	stóma (mouth)

τόπος	tópos (place)
φῶς	fos (light)
χέρι	héri (hand)
ψωμί	[1]psomí (bread)

1. x and ps at the beginning of a word should be pronounced in the same way as in tax or lips.

Groups of consonants

γγ	as **ng** in anger	ἀγγελία	angelía (notice)
γκ	as **g** in game	γκρεμός	gremós (precipice)
γξ	as **nx** in anxiety	φάλαγξ	fálanx (phalanx)
γχ	as **nh**	ἔγχρωμος	énhromos (coloured)
μπ	as **b** in bare	μπότα	bóta (boot)
μπ	as **mb** in member	λάμπα	lámba (lamp)
ντ	as **d** in dear	ντομάτα	domáta (tomato)
ντ	as **nd** in end	δέντρο	dhéndro (tree)
τζ	as **dz**	τζάκι	dzáki (fireplace)

STRESS

Unless written in capitals, almost all words (except for a few mono-syllabic ones whose accent is absorbed by the word that precedes them) are accented. Accents are indicated in this phrase book by **bold type** from this point on. Although there are three accents in Greek (ή, ή, ῆ) they all have the same value and make absolutely no difference to the pronunciation except in accenting the vowel of the syllable where they occur. Vowels at the beginning of a word, whether in capitals or lower case, also bear breathings (ή, ἡ) which should be ignored. The diaeresis is used to separate vowels which otherwise would form a group. The diaeresis is indicated by αϊ as in παϊδι paidhi (rib) as compared to παιδί pedhi (child).

PUNCTUATION

The comma and full stop are used as in English. The Greek semi-colon is a raised full stop (·) and the question mark is like the English semi-colon (;).

IDIOMS

There are two forms of modern Greek, the *dhemotiki* (demotic) which is the ordinary language spoken more or less throughout Greece (excepting for dialects) and the *katharevoussa* (purist) which is mainly used for official documents, school and university text-books and sometimes in newspapers. The *katharevoussa* is an artificial form of Greek closer to older forms in the evolution of modern Greek from classical Greek. This phrase book uses the ordinary demotic language which most people speak. For this reason neologisms and foreign words which have entered the ordinary Greek vocabulary have not been excluded. On the contrary, where a word is identical or similar to an English one, while it is also common in Greek usage, we have deliberately chosen to use it in preference to a more traditional Greek one.

It is common in Greek to address people one does not know personally in the formal polite form rather than the familiar, which means using verbs in the second person plural. Almost all phrases in this book are constructed in the polite form.

ESSENTIAL GRAMMAR

NOUNS AND ARTICLES

All Greek nouns are divided into three genders: masculine, feminine and neuter.

All nouns of all genders have cases according to their function in a sentence. In addition to the nominative there are also the genitive and the accusative. The genitive expresses possession; the accusative is used after prepositions and as the object of verbs. Articles take the same case as the noun to which they belong.

Singular

Masculine nouns are preceded by the definite article ὁ (o). Their indefinite article is ἕνας (enas). They are divided in three groups according to their endings which are -ος, -ας, -ης; e.g. ὁ θεός (o theos – the god), ὁ ἀέρας (o aeras – the wind), ὁ ἐργάτης (o erghatis – the worker).

			-ος		**-ας**		**-ης**	
nom.	ὁ	o	θεός	theos	ἀέρας	aeras	ἐργάτης	erghatis
gen.	τοῦ	tou	θεοῦ	theou	ἀέρα	aera	ἐργάτη	erghati
acc.	τόν	ton	θεό	theo	ἀέρα	aera	ἐργάτη	erghati

Feminine nouns are preceded by the definite article ἡ (i). Their indefinite article is μία (mia). They are divided into two groups according to their endings which are -η and -α; e.g. ἡ ψυχή (i psihi – the soul), ἡ θάλασσα, (i thalassa – the sea).

			-η		**-α**	
nom.	ἡ	i	ψυχή	psihi	θάλασσα	thalassa

| *gen.* | τῆς tis | ψυχῆς | psihis | θάλασσας | thalassas |
| *acc.* | τήν tin | ψυχή | psihi | θάλασσα | thalassa |

Neuter nouns are preceded by the definite article τό (to) and their indefinite article is ἕνα (ena). They end mostly in -ο, -α, and -ι; e.g. τό πλοῖο (to plio – the boat), τό δίπλωμα (to dhiploma – the diploma), τό τραγούδι (to traghoudhi – the song).

		-ο	**-α**	**-ι**
nom.	τό	πλοῖο	δίπλωμα	τραγούδι
		to plio	dhiploma	traghoudhi
gen.	τοῦ	πλοίου	διπλώματος	τραγουδιοῦ
		tou pliou	dhiplomatos	traghoudhiou
acc.	τό	πλοῖο	δίπλωμα	τραγούδι
		to plio	dhiploma	traghoudhi

Proper nouns also take an article and have cases, whether they are masculine, feminine, or neuter (some names of places only).

Plural

Masculine The article ὁ changes to οἱ. Masculine nouns ending in -ος change to -οι; those ending in -ας and -ης to -ες.

		-οι		**-ες**		**-ες**	
nom.	οἱ i	θεοί	thei	ἀέρες	aeres	ἐργάτες	erghates
gen.	τῶν ton	θεῶν	theon	ἀέρων	aeron	ἐργατῶν	erghaton
acc.	τούς tous	θεούς	theous	ἀέρες	aeres	ἐργάτες	erghates

Feminine The article ἡ changes to οἱ. The ending -η or -α changes to -ες. Some feminine nouns change the ending -η to -εις; e.g. ἡ πόλη (i poli – the town) becomes οἱ πόλεις (i polis – the towns); ἡ λέξη (i lexi – the word), οἱ λέξεις (i lexis – the words).

			-ες		**-εις**	
nom.	οἱ	i	ψυχές	psihes	πόλεις	polis
gen.	τῶν	ton	ψυχῶν	psihon	πόλεων	poleon
acc.	τίς	tis	ψυχές	psihes	πόλεις	polis

Neuter The article τό changes to τά. The ending -ο changes to -α, the ending -α to -ατα, the ending -ι to -ια.

		-α		**-ατα**		**-ια**
nom.	τά	πλοῖα	διπλώματα	τραγούδια
		ta plia	dhiplomata	traghoudhia
gen.	τῶν	πλοίων	διπλωμάτων	τραγουδιῶν
		ton plion	dhiplomaton	traghoudhion
acc.	τά	πλοῖα	διπλώματα	τραγούδια
		ta plia	dhiplomata	traghoudhia

ADJECTIVES

The endings of adjectives correspond to the three genders of the nouns they qualify. Masculine adjectives end in -ος (plural -οι), e.g. ὁ καλός – good. Feminine adjectives end in -η and some in -α (plural -ες); e.g. ἡ καλή – good. Neuter adjectives end in -ο (plural -α); e.g. τό καλό – good. Masculine, feminine and neuter adjectives have the same three cases (nominative, genitive and accusative) as the nouns they qualify.

For example:

	masculine	*feminine*	*neuter*
nom.	ὁ καλός o kalos	ἡ καλή i kali	τό καλό to kalo
gen.	τοῦ καλοῦ tou kalou	τῆς καλῆς tis kalis	τοῦ καλοῦ tou kalou
acc.	τόν καλό ton kalo	τήν καλή tin kali	τό καλό to kalo

Adjectives usually precede the nouns they qualify.

Possessive adjectives follow the nouns with which they are associated and they change for person and number. They are not stressed.

singular		*plural*	
μου	mou (my)	μας	mas (our)
σου	sou (your)	σας	sas (your)
του	tou (his)	τους	tous (their)
της	tis (hers)		
του	tou (its)		

ὁ ἄντρας μου o andras mou	(my husband)	οἱ ἄντρες μας i andres mas	(our husbands)
ἡ γυναίκα σου i ghineka sou	(your wife)	οἱ γυναῖκες σας i ghinekes sas	(your wives)
τό παιδί του (της) to pedhi tou (tis)	(his (her) child)	τά παιδιά τους ta pedhia tous	(their children)

PRONOUNS

Possessive pronouns have the same gender and number as the nouns
they replace.

masculine

singular		*plural*	
δικός μου	mine	δικός μας	ours
	(i.e. this dog is mine)		(i.e. this dog is ours)
δικός σου	yours	δικός σας	yours
δικός του	his	δικός τους	theirs
δικός της	hers		
δικός του	its		

feminine		*neuter*	
singular	*plural*	*singular*	*plural*
δική μου, etc	δικές μου	δικό μου, etc	δικό μου
(i.e. this chair is mine)		(i.e. this house is mine)	

In the case of plural possession (i.e. the possession of more than one
object) the masculine δικός changes to δικοί, the feminine δική to
δικές and the neuter δικό to δικά, just as with nouns.

δικοί μας   (i.e. these dogs are ours)
δικές μου   (i.e. these chairs are mine)
δικά του   (i.e. these houses are his)

Personal pronouns:

ἐγώ	egho	I	ἐμεῖς	emis	we
ἐσύ	essi	you	ἐσεῖς	essis	you

αὐτός	aftos	he	αὐτοί	afti	they
αὐτή	afti	she			
αὐτό	afto	it			

As the endings of verbs denote person it is not necessary to use the personal pronouns except for emphasis.

The object (accusative) pronouns:

τόν	ton	him	τούς	tous	them (*m*)
τήν	tin	her	τίς	tis	them (*f*)
τό	to	it	τά	ta	them (*n*)

Nouns which are used as objects of verbs can be replaced by the above pronouns.

VERBS

To be

present		past and imperfect		future	
εἶμαι	– I am	ἤμουν	– I was, etc.	θά εἶμαι	– I shall be
εἶσαι	– you are	ἤσουν	– you were	θά εἶσαι	– you will be
εἶναι	– he/she/ it is	ἦταν	– he/she/it was	θά εἶναι	– he/she/it will be
εἴμαστε	– we are	ἤμασταν	– we were	θά εἴμαστε	– we shall be
εἶσαστε	– you are	ἤσασταν	– you were	θά εἴσαστε	– you will be
εἶναι	– they are	ἦταν	– they were	θά εἶναι	– they will be

To have

present		past and imperfect		future	
ἔχω	– I have	εἶχα	– I had	θά ἔχω	– I shall have

ἔχεις	– you have	εἶχες	– you had	θά ἔχεις	– you will have
ἔχει	– he/she/it has	εἶχε	– he/she/it had	θά ἔχει	– he/she/it will have
ἔχουμε	– we have	εἴχαμε	– we had	θά ἔχουμε	– we shall have
ἔχετε	– you have	εἴχατε	– you had	θά ἔχετε	– you will have
ἔχουν	– they have	εἶχαν	– they had	θά ἔχουν	– they will have

Regular Verbs

Greek regular verbs may be *active*, ending in -ω in the first person singular of the present tense and denoting an action performed by the subject – or *passive*, ending in -μαι in the first person singular of the present tense and denoting an action received by the subject. This division, however, is only a general one and it does not necessarily apply in all cases. Most verbs have both active and passive forms.

The present tense corresponds to the English simple present and the present continuous (I do, I am doing).

active		*passive*	
πλένω	– I wash, etc.	πλένομαι	– I wash myself, etc.
πλένεις		πλένεσαι	
πλένει		πλένεται	
πλένουμε		πλενόμαστε	
πλένετε		πλενόσαστε	
πλένουν		πλένονται	

The future tense is formed by placing the particle θά in front of the indefinite which is otherwise never used by itself. By placing the particle θά in front of the present tense, one expresses the future continuous (I shall be doing). The indefinite is more or less the same as the English infinitive, but it is conjugated. As there are nine sub-classes of active verbs, depending on the way the indefinite is formed, and as it will be practically impossible for a user of this book to familiarize himself sufficiently with all the verbs that fall under these classes, it will be sufficient here to give only a few examples.

θά ἀρχίσω – I shall begin, etc.	θά δουλέψω – I shall work, etc.	θά κάνω – I shall make, etc.
θά ἀρχίσης	θά δουλέψης	θά κάνης
θά ἀρχίση	θά δουλέψη	θά κάνη
θά ἀρχίσωμε	θά δουλέψωμε	θά κάνωμε
θά ἀρχίσετε	θά δουλέψετε	θά κάνετε
θά ἀρχίσουν	θά δουλέψουν	θά κάνουν

The past tense is formed by changing the final -ω of the indefinite to -α. As in the case of the future tense, unless one is familiar with the indefinite forms, it is impossible to give a simple rule in forming the simple past.

The imperfect tense is formed by using the present, instead of the indefinite, but otherwise changing the ending as in the past

past	*imperfect*
ἄρχισα – I began, etc.	ἄρχιζα – I was beginning, etc.
ἄρχισες	ἄρχιζες

ἄρχισε	ἄρχιζε
ἀρχίσαμε	ἀρχίζαμε
ἀρχίσατε	ἀρχίζατε
ἄρχισαν	ἄρχιζαν

The perfect tenses are formed by the auxiliary verb ἔχω (I have) in the present and εἶχα (I had) in the past with the third person singular of the indefinite.

present perfect		*past perfect*	
ἔχω ἀρχίσει	– I have begun, etc.	εἶχα ἀρχίσει	– I had begun, etc.
ἔχεις ἀρχίσει		εἶχες ἀρχίσει	
ἔχει ἀρχίσει		εἶχε ἀρχίσει	
ἔχουμε ἀρχίσει		εἴχαμε ἀρχίσει	
ἔχετε ἀρχίσει		εἴχατε ἀρχίσει	
ἔχουν ἀρχίσει		εἶχαν ἀρχίσει	

The imperative form, which expresses command or request in the second person, is formed by changing the -ω of the indefinite into -ε.

ἀρχίσω	ἄρχισε
παίξω	παῖξε
γράψω	γράψε

PREPOSITIONS

σ' (σέ)	se	to (person)
στό	sto	to (direction), at
χωρίς	horís	without
γιά	ghia	for
πρός	pros	towards

πρίν	prin	before
μέ	me	with
ἀπό	apo	from
ὡς	os	until
μέχρι	mehri	until
μετά	meta	after
σάν	san	like
παρά	para	in spite of

πάνω στό	pano sto	on
κοντά στό	konta sto	near
μέσα στό	messa sto	in
γύρω στό	ghiro sto	around
μαζί μέ	mazi me	with
πάνω ἀπό	pano apo	over
κάτω ἀπό	kato apo	under
πίσω ἀπό	pisso apo	behind
γύρω σέ	ghiro se	around (time)
γύρω ἀπό	ghiro apo	round
ἔξω ἀπό	exo apo	outside of
πρίν ἀπό	prin apo	before
ὕστερα ἀπό	istera apo	after

FIRST THINGS

Essentials

Yes	Ναί ne
No	Ὄχι ohi
Please	Παρακαλῶ parakalo
Thank you	Εὐχαριστῶ efharisto
No, thank you	Ὄχι, εὐχαριστῶ ohi, efharisto

Questions and requests

Where is/are . . . ?	Ποῦ εἶναι . . . ; pou ine
When ?	Πότε; pote
How much is/are . . . ?	Πόσο κάνει/κάνουν . . . ; posso kani/kanoun

How far ?	Πόσο μακριά; posso makria
What's this ?	Τί εἶναι αὐτό; ti ine afto
What do you want ?	Τί θέλεις; ti thelis
What must I do ?	Τί πρέπει νά κάνω; ti prepi na kano
Have you .../do you sell ...?	Ἔχετε ...; ehete
Is there ...?	Ὑπάρχει ...; iparhi
Have you seen ...?	Ἔχετε δεῖ ...; ehete dhi
May I have ...?	Μπορῶ νά ἔχω ...; boro na eho
I want/should like ...	Θέλω/Θά ἤθελα ... thelo/tha ithela
I don't want ...	Δέν θέλω dhen thelo

Useful statements

Here is/are ...	Ἐδῶ εἶναι ... **edho ine**
I like it/them	Μ'ἀρέσει/μ'ἀρέσουν **maressi/maressoun**
I don't like it	Δέ μ' ἀρέσει **dhe maressi**
I know	Ξέρω **xero**
I don't know	Δέν ξέρω **dhen xero**
I didn't know	Δέν ἤξερα **dhen ixera**
I think so	Νομίζω **nomizo**
I'm hungry	Πεινῶ **pino**
I'm thirsty	Διψῶ **dhipso**
I'm tired	Εἶμαι κουρασμένος **ime kourasmenos**
I'm in a hurry	Βιάζομαι **viazome**

I'm ready	Εἶμαι ἔτοιμος
	ime etimos
Leave me alone	'Αφῆστε με ἥσυχο
	afiste me isiho
Just a moment	*Μιά στιγμή
	mia stighmi
This way, please	*'Απ' ἐδῶ παρακαλῶ
	apedho parakalo
Take a seat	*Καθίστε
	kathiste
Come in!	*'Εμπρός
	embros
It's cheap	Εἶναι φθηνό
	ine fthino
It's too expensive	Εἶναι πολύ ἀκριβό
	ine poli akrivo
That's all	Φτάνει
	ftani
You're right	Ἔχετε δίκιο
	ehete dhikio
You're wrong	Κάνετε λάθος
	kanete lathos

Language problems

I'm English/American	Εἶμαι Ἐγγλέζος/Ἀμερικάνος **ime englezos/amerikanos**
Do you speak English	Μιλᾶτε Ἀγγλικά; **milate anglika**
I don't speak Greek	Δέν μιλῶ Ἑλληνικά **dhen milo elinika**
I don't understand	Δέν καταλαβαίνω **dhen katalaveno**
Would you say that again, please?	Μπορεῖτε νά ἐπαναλάβετε παρακαλῶ; **borite na epanalavete parakalo**
Please speak slowly	Μπορεῖτε νά μιλήσετε πιό ἀργά σᾶς παρακαλῶ; **borite na milissete pio argha sas parakalo**
How do you say it in Greek?	Πῶς λέγεται στά Ἑλληνικά; **pos leghete sta elinika**

Polite phrases

Sorry	Συγγνώμη **sighnomi**

Excuse me	Μέ συγχωρῆτε me sinhorite
That's all right	Δέν πειράζει dhen pirazi
Don't mention it/You're welcome (*after thanks*)	Παρακαλῶ parakalo
Don't worry	Μήν ἀνησυχῆτε min anissihite
It doesn't matter	Δέν πειράζει dhen pirazi
I beg your pardon?	Τί εἴπατε; ti ipate
Am I disturbing you?	Μήπως σᾶς ἐνοχλῶ; mipos sas enohlo
I'm sorry to have troubled you	Μέ συγχωρῆτε γιά τήν ἐνόχληση me sinhorite ghia tin enohlissi
Good/that's fine	Καλά/ἐντάξει kala/entaxi
Thank you for your trouble	Σᾶς εὐχαριστῶ γιά τόν κόπο sas efharisto ghia ton **kopo**
That's nice/beautiful	ὄμορφο/Πολύ ὡραῖο omorfo/poli oreo

Greetings and hospitality

Good morning/good day	Καλημέρα σας kalimera sas
Good afternoon	Καλησπέρα σας kalispera sas
Good evening	Καλησπέρα σας kalispera sas
Good night	Καληνύχτα σας kalinihta sas
Hello	Γειά σας ghia sas
How are you?	Πῶς εἴσαστε; pos issaste
Very well, thank you	Πολύ καλά εὐχαριστῶ poli kala efharisto
Good-bye	Χαίρεται herete
See you soon	Εἰς τό ἐπανιδεῖν issto epanidhin
See you tomorrow	Θά ἰδωθοῦμε αὔριο tha idhothoume avrio
Have you met my wife?	Ἔχετε γνωρίσει τή γυναῖκα μου; ehete ghnorissi ti ghineka mou

This is my husband	Αὐτός εἶναι ὁ ἄντρας μου
	aftos ine o andras mou
May I introduce you to ...	Νά σᾶς συστήσω στόν/στήν ...
	na sas sistisso ston/stin
Glad to know you	Χαίρω πολύ
	hero poli
What's your name?	Πῶς ὀνομάζεστε;
	pos onomazeste
What's your address?	Ποιά εἶναι ἡ διεύθυνση σας;
	pia ine i dhiefthinssi sas
What's your telephone number?	Ποιό εἶναι τό τηλέφωνο σας;
	pio ine to tilefono sas
Where are you staying?	*Ποῦ μένετε;
	pou menete
Where are you from?	*᾽Από ποῦ εἴσαστε;
	apo pou issaste
Would you like a drink	*Θέλετε κάτι νά πιεῖτε;
	thelete kati na piite
Do you smoke?	*Καπνίζετε;
	kapnizete
Can I offer you anything?	*Τί μπορῶ νά σᾶς προσφέρω;
	ti boro na sas prosfero
Thanks for the inivitation	Εὐχαριστῶ γιά τή πρόσκληση
	efharisto ghia ti prosklissi
Are you doing anything this evening?	Τί κάνετε ἀπόψε;
	ti kanete apopse

Could we have coffee together?	Θέλετε νά συναντηθούμε γιά καφέ; thelete na sinantithoume ghia kafe
Could we have dinner together?	Θέλετε νά φᾶμε μαζί τό βράδυ; thelete na fame mazi to vradhi
Would you like to go to the museum/for a walk/dancing with me?	Θέλετε νά πᾶμε στό μουσεῖο/γιά ἕνα περίπατο/νά χορέψουμε; thelete na pame sto mousio/ghia ena peripato/na horepsoume
Bon voyage	Καλό ταξίδι kalo taxidhi
Good luck/all the best	Καλή τύχη/ὅτι ἐπιθυμεῖτε kali tihi/oti epithimite

SIGNS AND PUBLIC NOTICES[1]

Ἀνελκυστήρ anelkistir	Lift/elevator
Ἀνοικτό anikto	Open
Ἀπαγορεύεται ἡ εἴσοδος apaghorevete i issodhos	No entry
Ἀπαγορεύεται ἡ εἴσοδος apaghorevete i issodhos	No admission
Ἀπαγορεύεται τό κάπνισμα apaghorevete to kapnizma	No smoking
Ἀποχωρητήριο/Τουαλέτα apohoritirio/toualeta	Lavatory/toilet
Ἀστυνομία astinomia	Police station
Δωμάτιο πρός ἐνοικίασιν dhomatio pros enikiassin	Room to let
Εἴσοδος issodhos	Entrance
Εἴσοδος ἐλευθέρα issodhos elefthera	Admission free
Ἐλεύθερο elefthero	Vacant/free/unoccupied
Ἐνοικιάζεται enikiazete	To let

1. See also ROAD SIGNS (p. 59) and SIGNS TO LOOK FOR AT STATIONS (p. 42).

Ἔξοδος exodhos	Exit
Ἔξοδος κινδύνου exodhos kindhinou	Emergency exit
Ἰδιαίτερον idhieteron	Private
Κατειλημμένο katilimeno	Engaged/occupied
Κίνδυνος kindhinos	Danger
Κλειστό klisto	Closed
Κτυπῆστε τόν κόδωνα ktipiste ton kodhona	Ring
Κυρίων kirion	Gentlemen
Κυριῶν kirion	Ladies
Μεταφραστής metafrastis	Interpreter
Μή ἐγγίζετε mi engizete	Do not touch
Μή πόσιμο νερό mi possimo nero	Not for drinking
Μόνον ὄρθιοι monon orthii	Standing room only

Ὁδηγός   Guide
odhighos

Οἱ παραβάτες θά διωχθοῦν   Trespassers will be prosecuted
i paravates tha dhiohthoun

Ὅλο δεξιά   Keep right
olo dhexia

Παρακαλεῖστε ὅπως μή …   You are requested not to …
parakalisthe opos mi …

Πεζοί   Pedestrians
pezi

Πιασμένο/Κατειλημμένο   Reserved
piasmeno/katilimeno

Πλῆρες   House full (cinema, etc.)
plires

Πληροφορεῖες   Information
plirofories

Πόσιμο νερό   Drinking water
possimo nero

Προσοχή   Caution
prosohi

Ταμίας   Cashier
tamias

Ταχυδρομεῖο   Post office
tahidhromio

Τράπεζα   Bank
trapeza

MONEY[1]

Is there an exchange bureau near here?	Ποῦ εἶναι ἡ πλησιέστερη τράπεζα; pou ine i plissiesteri trapeza
Do you change travellers' cheques?	'Αλλάζετε travellers' cheques; allazete traveller's cheques
Where can I change travellers' cheques?	Ποῦ μπορῶ ν'ἀλλάξω travellers' cheques pou boro nalaxo travellers' cheques
I want to change some pounds/dollars	Θέλω ν'ἀλλάξω μερικές λίρες/δολλάρια thelo nalaxo merikes lires/dholaria
How much do I get for a pound/dollar?	Πόσες δραχμές στή λίρα/στό δολλάριο; posses dhrahmes sti lira/sto dholario
Can you give me some small change, please?	Μοῦ δίνετε μερικά ψιλά παρακαλῶ; mou dhinete merika psila parakalo
Sign here, please	*'Υπογράψτε ἐδῶ παρακαλῶ ipoghrapste edho parakalo
Go to the cashier	*Πηγαίνετε στό ταμεῖο pighenete sto tamio

1. Banks are open from 8.00 to 13.00, Monday to Saturday, although some branches in Athens open in the afternoon during the tourist season.

CURRENCY

100 Λεπτά = 1 Δραχμή/pl. Δραχμές
    lepta   drahmi   drahmes

TRAVEL

On Arrival

Customs	*Τελωνεῖον telonion
Passport control	*Ἔλεγχος διαβατηρίων elenhos dhiavatirion
Your passport, please	*Τό διαβατήριο σας παρακαλῶ to dhiavatirio sas parakalo
May I see your green card, please ?	*Τά χαρτιά ἀσφαλείας σας παρακαλῶ/τήν πράσινη κάρτα σας ta hartia asfalias parakale/tin prassini karta sas
Are you together ?	*Εἴσατε μαζί; issaste mazi
I'm travelling alone	Ταξιδεύω μόνος μου taxidhevo monos mou
I'm travelling with my wife/ a friend	Ταξιδεύω μέ τή γυναίκα μου/ ἕνα φίλο μου taxidhevo me ti ghineka mou/ ena filo mou
I'm here on business/on holiday	Ἔρχομαι γιά δουλειά/γιά διακοπές erhome ghia dhoulia/ghia dhiakopes

What is your address in . . ?	*Ποιά είναι ἡ διεύθυνση σας στήν . . . ; pia ine i dhiefthinssi sas stin
How long are you staying here?	*Πόσο θά μείνετε ἐδῶ; posso tha minete edho
How much money have you got?	*Πόσα χρήματα ἔχετε μαζί σας; possa hrimata ehete mazi sas
I have . . ./pounds/dollars	Ἔχω . . ./λίρες/δολλάρια eho . . ./lires/dholaria
Which is your luggage?	*Ποιές είναι οἱ ἀποσκευές σας; pies ine i aposkeves sas
Have you anything to declare?	*Ἔχετε τίποτα νά δηλώσετε; ehete tipota na dhilossete
This is my luggage	Αὐτές είναι οἱ ἀποσκευές μου aftes ine i aposkeves mou
I have only my personal things in it	Ἔχω μόνο εἴδη προσωπικῆς χρήσεως eho mono idhi prossopikis hrisseos
Open this bag, please	*Ἀνοῖξτε αὐτή τή βαλίτσα παρακαλῶ anixte afti ti valitsa parakalo
Can I shut my case now?	Μπορῶ νά κλείσω τή βαλίτσα μου τώρα; boro na klisso ti valitsa mou tora

May I go ?	Μπορῶ νά πηγαίνω; boro na pigheno
Where is the information bureau, please ?	Ποῦ εἶναι τό γραφεῖο πληροφο- ριῶν παρακαλῶ; pou ine to ghrafio pliroforion parakalo
Porter, here is my luggage	Ἀχθοφόρε, αὐτές εἶναι οἱ ἀποσκευές μου ahthofore, aftes ine i aposkeves mou
What's the price for each piece of luggage ?	Πόσα παίρνεις γιά κάθε βαλίτσα; possa pernis ghia kathe valitsa
I shall take this myself	Αὐτό θά τό κρατήσω afto tha to kratisso
That's not mine	Αὐτό δέν εἶναι δικό μου afto dhen ine dhiko mou
Would you call a taxi ?	Φωνάζεις ἕνα ταξί σέ παρα- καλῶ; fonazis ena taxi se parakalo
How much do I owe you ?	Πόσα σοῦ ὀφείλω; possa sou ofilo

Buying a ticket

Where's the nearest travel agency ?	Ποῦ εἶναι τό πλησιέστερο γραφεῖο ταξιδιῶν; **pou ine to plissiestero ghrafio taxidhion**
Have you a timetable, please ?	Ἔχετε ἕνα δρομολόγειο παρακαλῶ; **ehete ena dhromologhio parakalo**
What's the tourist return fare to . . . ?	Πόσο κάνει ἕνα εἰσιτήριο μετ'ἐπιστροφῆς τουριστικῆς θέσεως γιά . . .; **posso kani ena issitirio metepistrofis touristikis thesseos ghia**
How much is it first class to . . . ?	Πόσο στοιχίζει πρώτη θέση γιά . . .; **posso stihizi proti thessi ghia**
A second class ticket to . . .	Ἕνα εἰσιτήριο δευτέρας θέσεως γιά . . . **ena issitirio dhefteras thesseos ghia**
Three tickets to . . .	Τρία εἰσιτήρια γιά . . . **tria issitiria ghia**

A day return to . . .	Ένα εἰσιτήριο μετ'ἐπιστροφῆς κατά τή διάρκεια τῆς ἡμέρας γιά . . .
	ena issitirio metepistrofis kata ti dhiarkia tis imeras ghia
How long is this ticket valid?	Γιά πόσο ἰσχύει αὐτό τό εἰσιτήριο;
	ghia posso ishii afto to issitirio
Must I book in advance?	Εἶναι ἀπαραίτητο νά κλείσω θέση ἐκ τῶν προτέρων;
	ine aparetito na klisso thessi ek ton proteron

Signs to look for at stations, termini, etc.

Arrivals	Ἀφίξεις
	afixis
Booking office	Γραφεῖον εἰσιτηρίων
	ghrafion issitirion
Buses	Λεωφορεῖα
	leoforia
Connections	Ἀνταποκρίσεις
	antapokrissis
Departures	Ἀναχωρήσεις
	anahorissis

Enquiries	Πληροφορίαι pliriforie
Exchange	Τράπεζα trapeza
Gentlemen	Κυρίων kirion
Ladies' room	Κυριῶν kirion
Luggage	Ἀποσκευαί aposkeve
Lost Property	Χαμένα ἀντικείμενα hamena antikimena
Main Lines	Κύριες γραμμές kiries ghrames
Non-Smoker	Ἀπαγορεύεται τό κάπνισμα apaghorevete to kapnizma
Refreshments	Ἀναψυκτικά anapsiktika
Reservations	Κρατήσεις kratissis
Smoker	Ἐπιτρέπεται τό κάπνισμα epitrepete to kapnizma
Suburban Lines	Γραμμές περιχώρων ghrames perihoron
Taxis	Ταξί taxi

Tickets	Εἰσιτήρια issitíria
Underground	Ὑπόγειος ipoghios
Waiting Room	Αἴθουσα ἀναμονῆς ethoussa anamonis

By train and underground[1]

RESERVATIONS AND INQUIRIES

Where's the railway station?	Ποῦ εἶναι ὁ σιδηροδρομικός σταθμός; pou ine o sidhirodhromikos stathmos
Two seats on the 11.15 tomorrow to ...	Δύο θέσεις γιά τό τραῖνο τῶν ἕνδεκα καί τέταρτο αὔριο γιά ... dhio thessis ghia to treno ton endheka ke tetarto avrio ghia
I want to reserve a sleeper	Θέλω νά κρατήσω μία couchette thelo na kratisso mia couchette

1. For help in understanding the answers to these and similar questions see TIMES AND DATES (p. 168), NUMBERS (p. 174), DIRECTIONS (p. 55).

How much does a couchette cost ?	Πόσο στοιχίζει ἡ couchette; posso stihizi i couchette
I want to register this luggage through to ...	Θέλω νά στείλω αὐτές τίς ἀποσκευές συστημένες στό... thelo na stilo aftes tis aposkeves sistimenes sto
Is it an express or a local train ?	Εἶναι ταχεία ἡ τοπικό τραῖνο; ine tahia i topiko treno
Is there an earlier/later train ?	Ὑπάρχει κανένα τραῖνο πιό νωρίς/ἀργότερα; iparhi kanena treno pio noris/ arghotera
Is there a restaurant car on the train ?	Ὑπάρχει ἑστιατόριο στό τραῖνο; iparhi estiatorio sto treno

CHANGING

Is there a through train to ...?	Ὑπάρχει τραῖνο κατ'εὐθεῖαν γιά...; iparhi treno katefthian ghia
Do I have to change?	Πρέπει ν'ἀλλάξω; prepi nalaxo
Where do I change?	Ποῦ πρέπει ν'ἀλλάξω; pou prepi nalaxo
What time is there a connection to ... ?	Τί ὥρα ἔχει ἀνταπόκριση γιά τό...; ti ora ehi antapokrissi ghia to

DEPARTURE

When does the train leave?

Πότε φεύγει τό τραῖνο;
pote fevghi to treno

Which platform does the train to ... leave from?

'Από ποῦ φεύγει τό τραῖνο γιά τό ...;
apo pou fevghi to treno ghia to

Is this the train for ...?

Εἶναι αὐτό τό τραῖνο γιά τό ...;
ine afto to treno ghia to

ARRIVAL

When does it get to ...?

Πότε φθάνει στό ...;
pote fthani sto

Does the train stop at ...?

Σταματάει τό τραῖνο στό ...;
stamatai to treno sto

How long do we stop here?

Πόση ὥρα σταματάει τό τραῖνο ἐδῶ;
possi ora stamatai to treno edho

Is the train late?

Ἔχει ἀργοπορία τό τραῖνο;
ehi arghoporia to treno

When does the train from ... get in?

Τί ὥρα φθάνει τό τραῖνο ἀπό ...;
ti ora fthani to treno apo

At which platform?

Σέ ποιά πλατφόρμα;
se pia platforma

ON THE TRAIN

We have reserved seats

Ἔχουμε πιασμένες θέσεις
ehoume piasmenes thessis

Is this seat free?	Εἶναι ἐλεύθερη αὐτή ἡ θέση; ine eleftheri afti i thessi
This seat is taken	Αὐτή ἡ θέση εἶναι πιασμένη afti i thessi ine piasmeni

---

By air

Where's the Olympic office?	Ποῦ εἶναι τά γραφεῖα τῆς 'Ολυμπιακῆς; pou ine ta ghrafia tis olimbiakis
I'd like to book two seats on Monday's plane to . . .	Θέλω νά κλείσω δύο θέσεις γιά τό . . . τή Δευτέρα thelo na klisso dhio thessis ghia to . . . ti dheftera
Is there a flight to . . . next Thursday?	Ὑπάρχει πτήσις γιά τό . . . τήν ἐρχόμενη Πέμπτη; iparhi ptissis ghia to . . . tin erhomeni pempti
When does it leave/arrive?	Πότε φεύγει/φθάνει; pote fevghi/fthani
When does the next plane leave?	Πότε φεύγει τό ἐπόμενο ἀεροπλάνο; pote fevghi to epomeno aero- plano

Is there a coach to the airport?	Ὑπάρχει λεωφορεῖο γιά τό ἀεροδρόμιο;
	iparhi leoforio ghia to aerodhromio
When must I check in?	Πότε πρέπει νά παρουσιαστῶ;
	pote prepi na paroussiasto
Please cancel my reservation to . . .	Παρακαλῶ ἀκυρῶστε τήν κράτηση μου γιά . . .
	parakalo akiroste tin kratissi mou ghia
I'd like to change my reservation to . . .	Θέλω ν'ἀλλάξω τήν κράτηση μου γιά . . .
	thelo nalaxo tin kratissi mou ghia

By ship

Is there a boat/car ferry from here to . . . ?	Ὑπάρχει πλοῖο/ferry αὐτοκινήτων ἀπ'ἐδῶ στό . . . ;
	iparhi plio/ferry aftokiniton apedho sto
How long does it take to get to . . . ?	Πόσο παίρνει νά πάει κανείς στό . . . ;
	posso perni na pai kanis sto
How often do the boats leave?	Πόσο συχνά φεύγουν τά πλοῖα;
	poso sihna fevghoun ta plia

Where does the boat put in?	Πού πιάνει τό πλοῖο; pou piani to plio
Does it call at . . . ?	Σταματάει στό . . .; stamatai sto
When does the next boat leave?	Πότε φεύγει τό ἐπόμενο πλοῖο; pote fevghi to epomeno plio
Can I book a single berth cabin?	Μπορῶ νά κλείσωμ ία μονή καμπίνα; boro na klisso mia moni kabina
How many berths are there in this cabin?	Πόσα κρεββάτια ἔχει αὐτή ἡ καμπίνα; possa krevatia ehi afti i kabina
When must we go on board?	Πότε πρέπει νά ἐπιβιβαστοῦμε; pote prepi na epivivastoume
When do we dock?	Πότε πλευρίζουμε; pote plevrizoume
How long do we stay in port?	Πόση ὥρα θά μείνουμε στό λιμάνι; possi ora tha minoume sto limani

By bus or coach

Where's the bus station?	Ποῦ εἶναι ὁ σταθμός τῶν λεωφορείων; pou ine o stathmos ton leoforion
Bus stop	*στάσις λεωφορείου stassis leoforiou
When does the coach leave?	Πότε φεύγει τό λεωφορεῖο; pote fevghi to leoforio
What time do we get to ...	Πότε φθάνουμε στό ...; pote fthanoume sto
What stops does it make?	Ποῦ σταματάει; pou stamatai
Is it a long journey?	Εἶναι μακρύ ταξίδι; ine makri taxidhi
We want to make a sight-seeing tour round the city	Θέλουμε νά ἐπισκεφτοῦμε τά ἀξιοθέατα τῆς πόλης theloume na episkeftoume ta axiotheata tis polis
Is there an excursion to ... tomorrow?	Ὑπάρχει ἐκδρομή γιά τό ...αὔριο; iparhi ekdhromi ghia to ... avrio

What time is the next bus?	Πότε φεύγει τό ἐπόμενο λεωφορεῖο; pote fevghi to epomeno leoforio
Has the last bus gone?	Πέρασε τό τελευταῖο λεωφορεῖο; perasse to telefteo leoforio
Does this bus go to the centre?	Πηγαίνει στό κέντρο αὐτό τό λεωφορεῖο; pigheni sto kentro afto to leoforio
Does this bus go to the beach?	Πηγαίνει αὐτό τό λεωφορεῖο στή παραλία; pigheni afto to leoforio sti paralia
Does this bus go to the station?	Πηγαίνει αὐτό τό λεωφορεῖο στόν σταθμό; pigheni afto to leoforio ston stathmo
Does it go near . . . ?	Πηγαίνει κοντά . . . ; pigheni konta
Where can I get a bus to . . . ?	Ἀπό ποῦ μπορῶ νά πάρω τό λεωφορεῖο γιά . . . ; apo pou boro na paro to leoforio ghia
I want to go to . . .	Θέλω νά πάω στό . . . thelo na pao sto
Where do I get off?	Ποῦ πρέπει νά βγῶ; pou prepi na vgho

The bus to ... stops over there	*Τό λεωφορείο γιά τό ... σταματάει ἐκεῖ to leoforio ghia to ... stamatai eki
A number 30 goes to ...	*Τό τριάντα πηγαίνει στό ... to trianta pigheni sto
You must take a number 24	*Πρέπει νά πάρετε τό εἴκοσι τέσσερα prepi na parete to ikossitessera
You get off at the next stop	*Θά βγῆτε στήν ἐπόμενη στάση tha vghite stin epomeni stassi
The buses run every ten minutes/ every hour	*Τά λεωφορεῖα περνοῦν κάθε δέκα λεπτά/κάθε ὥρα ta leoforia pernoun kathe dheka lepta/kathe ora

By taxi

Are you free?	Ἐλεύθερος; eleftheros

Please take me to Hotel Central/ the station/this address	Μπορεῖς νά μέ πᾶς σέ παρακαλῶ στό Κεντρικό Ξενοδοχεῖο/ στόν σταθμό/σ᾽αὐτή τή διεύθυνση; boris na me pas se parakalo sto kentriko xenodhohio/sto stathmo/safti ti dhiefthinssi
Can you hurry, I'm late?	Σέ παρακαλῶ κάνε γρήγορα γιατί ἔχω ἀργήσει se parakalo kane ghrighora ghiati eho arghissi
I want to go through the centre	Θέλω νά περάσω ἀπ᾽τό κέντρο thelo na perasso apto kentro
Please wait a minute	Περίμενε σέ παρακαλῶ μιά στιγμή perimene se parakalo mia stighmi
Stop here	Σταμάτα ἐδῶ stamata edho
Is it far?	Εἶναι μακριά; ine makria
How much do you charge by the hour/for the day?	Πόσα παίρνεις μέ τήν ὥρα/τή μέρα; possa pernis me tin ora/ti mera
I'd like to go to . . . How much would you charge?	Θέλω νά πάω στό . . . Πόσα θά πάρεις; thelo na pao sto . . . possa tha paris

How much is it?	Πόσο είναι; posso ine
That's too much	Είναι πάρα πολύ ine parapoli
I am not prepared to spend that much	Δέν είμαι διατεθειμένος νά ξοδέψω τόσα πολλά dhen ime dhiatethimenos na ksodhepso tossa pola
It's a lot, but all right	Πολλά είναι, άλλά έν τάξει pola ine, ala endaxi

DIRECTIONS

Where is . . . ?	Ποῦ εἶναι; pou ine
Is this the way to . . . ?	Αὐτός εἶναι ὁ δρόμος γιά . . . ; aftos ine o dhromos ghia
Which is the road for . . . ?	Ποιός εἶναι ὁ δρόμος γιά . . . ; pios ine o dhromos ghia
How far is it to . . . ?	Πόσο ἀπέχει . . . ; posso apehi
How many kilometres ?	Πόσα χιλιόμετρα; possa hiliometra
We want to get on to the motorway to . . .	Θέλουμε νά πάρουμε τόν αὐτοκινητόδρομο γιά . . . theloume na paroume ton aftokinitodhromo ghia
Which is the best road to . . . ?	Ποιός εἶναι ὁ καλύτερος δρόμος γιά . . . ; pios ine o kaliteros dhromos ghia
Is it a good road ?	Εἶναι καλός δρόμος; ine kalos dhromos
Is it a motorway ?	Εἶναι αὐτοκινητόδρομος; ine aftokinitodhromos
Will we get to . . . by evening ?	Θά φθάσουμε στό . . . μέχρι τό βράδυ; tha fthassoume sto . . . mehri to vradhi

Where are we now ?	Ποῦ εἴμαστε τώρα; **pou imaste tora**
Please show me on the map	Δεῖξτε μου σᾶς παρακαλῶ στόν χάρτη **dhixte mou sas parakalo sto harti**
It's that way	*Εἶναι ἀπ'ἐδῶ **ine apedho**
It isn't far	*Δέν εἶναι μακριά **dhen ine makria**
Follow this road for 5 kilometres	*Ἀκολουθῆστε αὐτό τόν δρόμο γιά πέντε χιλιόμετρα **akolouthiste afto to dhromo ghia pente hiliometra**
Keep straight on	*Προχωρῆστε ἴσια **prohoriste issia**
Turn right at the crossroads	*Στρίψτε δεξιά στό σταυροδρόμι **stipste dhexia sto stavrodhromi**
Take the second road on the left	*Πάρτε τόν δεύτερο δρόμο ἀριστερά **parte ton dheftero dhromo aristera**
Turn right at the traffic-lights	*Στρίψτε δεξιά στά φῶτα κυκλοφορείας **stripste dhexia sta fota kikloforias**

Turn left after the bridge

*Στρίψτε ἀριστερά μετά τή
    γέφυρα
stripste aristera meta ti
    ghefira

The best road is the . . .

*Ὁ καλύτερος δρόμος εἶναι . . .
o kaliteros dhromos ine

Take this road as far as . . . and ask
    again

*Πάρτε αὐτόν τόν δρόμο μέχρι . . .
    καί ξαναρωτῆστε
parte afton ton dhromo
    mehri . . . ke xanarotiste

MOTORING

Where can I hire a car?

Ποῦ μπορῶ νά νοικιάσω ἕνα αὐτοκίνητο;
pou boro na nikiasso ena aftokinito

I want to hire a car and a driver/ a self drive car

Θέλω νά νοικιάσω ἕνα αὐτοκίνητο μέ σωφέρ/χωρίς σωφέρ
thelo na nikiasso ena aftokinito me sofer/horis sofer

How much is it by the hour/day/ week?

Πόσο κάνει τήν ὥρα/μέρα/ ἑβδομάδα;
posso kani tin ora/mera/ evdhomadha

Have you a road map, please?

Ἔχετε ἕναν ὁδικό χάρτη παρακαλῶ;
ehete enan odhiko harti parakalo

Where is a car park?

Ποῦ ἔχει χῶρο γιά παρκάρισμα;
pou ehi horo ghia parkarisma

Can I park here?

Μπορῶ νά παρκάρω ἐδῶ;
boro na parkaro edho

How long can I park here?

Πόση ὥρα μπορῶ νά παρκάρω ἐδῶ;
possi ora boro na parkaro edho

May I see your licence, please ?	*Μπορῶ νά δῶ τήν ἄδεια σας παρακαλῶ; boro na dho tin adhia sas parakalo

---

Road signs

Ἀδιέξοδος adhiexodhos	Dead end
Ἀπαγορεύεται ἡ εἴσοδος apaghorevete i issodhos	No entry
Ἀπαγορεύεται ἡ προσπέρασις apaghorevete i prosperassis	Overtaking prohibited
Ἀπαγορεύεται ἡ στάθμευσις apaghorevete i stathmefssis	No parking
Ἀπότομος λόφος apotomos lofos	Steep hill
Δρόμος κλειστός dhromos klistos	Road blocked
Δρόμος κλειστός dhromos klistos	Road closed
Ἐπιτρέπεται ἡ στάθμευσις epitrepete i stathmefssis	Parking allowed

Εὐθεία efthia	Get in lane
Κίνδυνος kindhinos	Danger
Μονόδρομος monodhromos	One way street
Ὁδηγῆτε μέ προσοχή odhighite me prosohi	Drive with care
Ὁδικά ἔργα odhika ergha	Road works ahead
Ὅλο δεξιά olo dhexia	Keep right
Ὅριον ταχύτητος orion tahititos	Speed limit
Παρέκκλισις pareklissis	Diversion
Σταματῆστε stamatiste	Stop
Στροφές strofes	Winding road

At the garage

Where is the nearest petrol station ?	Πού εἶναι τό πλησιέστερο βενζινάδικο; pou ine to plisiestero venzinadhiko
How far is the next petrol station ?	Πόσο ἀπέχει τό ἑπόμενο βενζινάδικο; posso apehi to epomeno venzinadhiko
Three gallons of petrol, and please check the oil and water	Τρία γαλλόνια βενζίνη καί παρακαλῶ κοιτᾶξτε τό λάδι καί τό νερό tria ghalonia venzini ke parakalo kitaxte to ladhi ke to nero
Fill her up	Γεμίστε το ghemiste to
How much is petrol a gallon ?	Πόσο κάνει τό γαλλόνι ἡ βενζίνη; posso kani to ghaloni i venzini
The oil needs changing	Τό λάδι θέλει ἄλλαγμα to ladhi theli alaghma

Check the tyre pressure, please[1]	Κοιτᾶξτε τόν ἀέρα στά λάστιχα παρακαλῶ kitaxte ton aera sta lastiha parakalo
Please change the tyre	'Αλλᾶξτε τό λάστιχο παρακαλῶ alaxte to lastiho parakalo
This tyre is punctured	Αὐτό τό λάστιχο τρύπησε afto to lastiho tripisse
The valve is leaking	Ἡ βαλβίδα τρέχει i valvidha trehi
The radiator is leaking	Τό καλοριφέρ τρέχει to kalorifer trehi
Please wash the car	Παρακαλῶ πλύντε τ'αὐτοκίνητο paraklo plinte t'aftokinito
Can I garage the car here?	Μπορῶ νά βάλλω τ'αὐτοκίνητο σ'αὐτό ἐδῶ τό γκαράζ; boro na valo t'aftokinito safto edho to garaz
What time does the garage close?	Τί ὥρα κλείνει τό γκαράζ; ti ora klini to garaz

1. See p. 76.

Repairs, etc.

Have you a breakdown service?	Κάνετε διορθώσεις; **kanete dhiorthossis**
Is there a mechanic?	Ὑπάρχει μηχανικός; **iparhi mihanikos**
My car's broken down, can you send someone to tow it?	Χάλασε τ'αὐτοκίνητο μου. Μπορεῖτε νά στείλετε κάποιον νά τό ριμουλκίσει; **halasse t'aftokinitomou. borite na stilete kapion na to rimoulkissi**
I want the car serviced	Θέλω νά μοῦ κάνετε συντήρηση τοῦ αὐτοκινήτου **thelo na mou kanete sintirissi tou aftokinitou**
The battery is flat, it needs charging	Ἡ μπαταρία εἶναι ἄδεια. Θέλει γέμισμα **i bataria ine adhia. theli ghemisma**

I've lost my car key	Ἔχασα τό κλειδί τοῦ αὐτονήκι- του μου
	ehassa to klidhi tou aftokinitou mou
The lock is broken/jammed	Ἡ κλειδαριά εἶναι σπασμένη/ κόλλησε
	i klidharia ine spasmeni/ kolisse
My car won't start	Δέν ξεκινάει τ'αὐτοκίνητο μου
	dhen ksekinai t'aftokinito mou
It's not running properly	Δέν λειτουργεῖ κανονικά
	dhen litourghi kanonika
The engine is overheating	Παραζεσταίνεται ἡ μηχανή
	parazestenete i mihani
The engine is firing badly	Ἡ μηχανή δέν τραβάει
	i mihani dhen travai
The engine knocks	Χτυπάει ἡ μηχανή
	htipai i mihani
Can you change this plug?	Μπορεῖτε ν'ἀλλάξετε αὐτή τή βαλβίδα;
	borite n'alaxete afti ti valvidha
There's a petrol/oil leak	Τρέχει ἡ βενζίνη/τό λάδι
	trehi i venzini/to ladhi
There's a smell of petrol/rubber	Μυρίζει βενζίνη/λάστιχο
	mirizi venzini/lastiho

The radiator is blocked/leaking	Τό καλοριφέρ εἶναι βουλωμένο/ τρέχει to kalorifer ine voulomeno/ trehi
Something is wrong with my car/ the engine/ the lights/the clutch/ the gearbox/ the brakes/the steering	Κάτι ἔχει τ'αὐτοκίνητο μου/ἡ μηχανή/τά φῶτα/ὁ συμπλέκτης/οἱ ταχύτητες/ τά φρένα/τό τιμόνι kati ehi t'aftokinitomou/i mihani/ta fota/o simplektis/ i tahitites/ ta frena/to timoni
There's a squeak/whine/rumble/ rattle	τρίζει κάνει ἕναν θόρυβο/μιά βοή/ἕναν κρότο trizi kani ena thorivo/mia voi/ ena kroto
It's a high/low noise	Εἶναι ἕνας ὀξύς/χαμηλός θόρυβος ine enas oxis/hamilos thorivos
It's intermittent/continuous	Εἶναι διακεκομμένος/συνεχής ine dhiakekomenos/sinehis
The carburettor needs adjusting	Τό καρμπιρατέρ πρέπει νά ρυθμιστεῖ to karbirater prepi na rithmisti
Can you repair it?	Μπορεῖτε νά τό διορθώσετε; borite na to dhiorthossete

How long will it take to repair?	Πόσο θά σᾶς πάρη νά τό διορθώσετε; posso tha sas pari na to dhiorthossete
What will it cost?	Τί θά στοιχίση; ti tha stihissi
When can I pick the car up?	Πότε μπορῶ νά πάρω τ'αὐτοκίνητο; pote boro na paro t'aftokinito
I need it as soon as possible	Τό χρειάζομαι ὅσο τό δυνατόν συντομώτερα to hriazome osso to dhinaton sintomotera
I need it in three hours/tomorrow morning	Τό χρειάζομαι σέ τρεῖς ὧρες/αὔριο τό πρωί to hriazome se tris ores/avrio to proi
It will take two days	*Θά πάρη δύο μέρες tha pari dhio meres
We can repair it temporarily	*Μποροῦμε νά τό ἐπιδιορθώσουμε προσωρινά boroume na to epidhiorthossoume prossorina
We haven't the right spares	*Δέν ἔχουμε τά κατάλληλα ἀνταλλακτικά dhen ehoume ta katalila antalaktika

We have to send for the spares	*Πρέπει νά παραγγείλουμε τ'ἀνταλλακτικά prepi na parangiloume t'antalaktika
You will need a new ...	*Χρειάζεστε ἕνα καινούργιο ... hriazeste ena kenourghio

---

Parts of a car and other vocabulary useful in a garage

---

accelerate (to)	Πατῶ τό γκάζι pato to gazi
accelerator	Γκάζι gazi
alignment	"Ενωση enossi
alternator	Μετασχηματιστής metakshimatistis
anti-freeze	'Αντιψυκτικό antipsiktiko
automatic transmission	Αὐτόματη μεταλλαγή aftomati metalaghi
axle	"Αξων τροχοῦ axon trohou

axleshaft	'Ακτίνα άξονος **aktina axonos**
battery	Μπαταρία **bataria**
beam	'Ακτίνα **aktina**
bonnet/hood	καπώ **kapo**
boot/truck	Πόρτ μπαγκάζ **port bagaz**
brake	Φρένο **freno**
disc brakes	Δισκόφρενα **dhiskofrena**
drum brakes	'Αερόφρενα **aerofrena**
footbrake	Ποδόφρενο **podhofreno**
handbrake	Χειρόφρενο **hirofreno**
brake fluid	'Υγρό φρένων **ighro frenon**
brake lights	Φῶτα φρένων **fota frenon**
breakdown	Χάλασε **halasse**

bumper	Προφυλακτήρ **profilaktir**
carburettor	Καρμπιρατέρ **karbirater**
carwash	Πλύσιμο **plissimo**
choke	Βαλβίδα ἀέρος καρμπιρατέρ **valvida aeros karbirater**
clutch	Συμπλέκτης **simplektis**
clutch plate	Δίσκος συμπλέκτου **dhiskos simplektou**
coil	Σύρμα **sirma**
condenser	Συμπηκνωτής **simpiknotis**
crankshaft	μανιβέλλα **manivela**
cylinder	Κύλινδρος **kilindhros**
differential gear	Διαφορική ταχύτης **dhiaforiki tahitis**
dip stick	Λαδόμετρο **ladhometro**
distilled water	᾿Απεσταγμένο νερό **apestaghmeno nero**

distributor	Διανομεύς dhianomefs
door	Πόρτα porta
doorhandle	Χερούλι herouli
drive (to)	'Οδηγῶ odhigho
driver	'Οδηγός odhighos
dynamo	Δυναμό dhinamo
electrical trouble	'Ηλεκτρική βλάβη ilektriki vlavi
engine	Μηχανή mihani
exhaust	'Εξάτμιση exatmissi
fan	'Ανεμιστήρας anemistiras
fanbelt	Λουρίδα ἀνεμιστῆρος louridha anemistiros
foglamp	Φῶς ὁμίχλης fos omihlis
fusebox	'Ασφάλειες asfalies

gear	Ταχύτης
	tahitis
gear box	Κιβώτιο ταχυτήτων
	kivotio tahititon
gear lever	Μοχλός ταχυτήτων
	mohlos tahititon
grease (to)	Λίπος
	lipos
headlights	Φανοί
	fani
heater	Καλοριφέρ
	kalorifer
horn	Κλάξον
	klaxon
hose	Σωλήνας
	solinas
ignition	Μίζα
	miza
ignition coil	Σύρμα μίζας
	sirma mizas
ignition key	Κλειδί μίζας
	klidhi mizas
indicator	Δείκτης
	dhiktis
inner tube	Ἐσωτερικός σωλήνας
	esoterikos solinas

jack	Γερανός
	gheranos
lights	Φῶτα
	fota
lock/catch	Κλειδαριά
	klidharia
mechanical trouble	Μηχανική βλάβη
	mihaniki vlavi
mirror	Καθρέπτης
	kathreptis
number plate	'Αριθμός
	arithmos
nut	Παξιμάδι
	paximadhi
oil	Λάδι
	ladhi
oil pressure	Πίεση λαδιοῦ
	piessi ladhiou
overdrive	'Υπερθέρμανση
	iperthermanssi
parking lights	Φῶτα σταθμεύσεως
	fota stathmefsseos
petrol	βενζίνη
	venzini
petrol can	Δοχεῖο βενζίνης
	dhohio venzinis

petrol pump	Ἀντλία βενζίνης antlia venzinis
petrol tank	Ντεπόζιτο βενζίνης depozito venzinis
piston	Πιστόνι pistoni
piston ring	Δακτύλιος πιστονιοῦ dhaktilios pistoniou
points	Σημεῖα ἐπαφῆς simia epafis
propeller shaft	Ἄξων axon
puncture	Τρύπημα λαστίχου tripima lastihou
radiator	Καλοριφέρ kalorifer
rear axle	Πίσω ἄξονας pisso axonas
rear lights	Πίσω φῶτα pisso fota
reverse (to)	Κάνω ὄπισθεν kano opisthen
reverse	Ὄπισθεν opisthen
roof-rack	Σχάρα skhara

seat	Θέση thessi
shock absorber	Σουσπανσιόν souspansion
sidelights	Πλαϊνά φῶτα plaina fota
silencer	Καταθιγαστής katassighastis
spanner	Κλειδί klidhi
spares	Ἀνταλλακτικά antalaktika
spare wheel	Ἀνταλλακτικό λάστιχο antalaktiko lastiho
(sparking) plug	Ἠλεκτρικός σπινθήρ ilektrikos spinthir
speed	Ταχύτης tahitis
speedometer	Δείκτης ταχύτητος dhiktis tahititos
spring	Ἐλατήριο elatirio
stall (to)	Σταματῶ stamato
starter	Μίζα miza

steering	'Οδήγησις odhighissis
steering wheel	Τιμόνι timoni
sunroof	Καπώ kapo
switch	Διακόπτης dhiakoptis
tank	Ντεπόζιτο depozito
tappets	Μπουλόνια boulonia
transmission	Μεταφορά metafora
tyre	Λάστιχο lastiho
tyre pressure	Πίεσις λαστίχου piessis lastihou
valve	Βαλβίδα valvidha
water pump	'Αντλία νεροῦ andlia nerou
wheel	Τροχός trohos
window	Παράθυρο parathiro

windscreen	Μπροστινό τζάμι brostino dzami
windscreen washers	Πλυντῆρες τζαμιῶν plindires dzamion
windscreen wipers	Καθαριστῆρες τζαμιῶν katharistires dzamion
wing	Φτερό ftero

Tyre pressure

type pressure

Πίεση ἀέρος στό λάστιχο
piessi aeros sto lastiho

lb. per sq. in.	kg. per sq. cm.	lb. per sq. in.	kg. per sq. cm.
16	1·1	36	2·5
18	1·3	39	2·7
20	1·4	40	2·8
22	1·5	43	3·0
25	1·7	45	3·2
29	2·0	46	3·2
32	2·3	50	3·5
35	2·5	60	4·2

A rough way to convert lb. per sq. in. to kg. per sq. cm.: multiply by 7 and divide by 100.

ACCOMMODATION[1]

Booking a room

Rooms to let	*'Ενοικιάζονται δωμάτια enikiazonte dhomatia
No vacancies	*Πλῆρες plires
Have you a room for the night?	"Εχετε ἕνα δωμάτιο γιά ἀπόψε; ehete ena dhomatio ghia apopse
I've reserved a room; my name is . . .	"Εχω κρατήσει ἕνα δωμάτιο. 'Ονομάζομαι . . . eho kratissi ena dhomatio. onomazome
Can you suggest another hotel?	Ξέρετε κανένα ἄλλο ξενοδοχεῖο; xerete kanena alo xenodhohio
I want a single room with a shower	Θέλω ἕνα μονό δωμάτιο μέ ντούς thelo ena mono dhomatio me douche
We want a room with a double bed and a bathroom	Θέλουμε ἕνα δωμάτιο μ'ἕνα διπλό κρεββάτι καί μπάνιο theloume ena dhomatio m'ena dhiplo krevati ke banio

1. See also LAUNDRY (p. 130) and RESTAURANT (p. 88).

Have you a room with twin beds ?	Ἔχετε ἕνα δωμάτιο μέ δύο κρεββάτια; ehete ena dhomatio me dhio krevatia
I want a room for two or three days/a week/until Friday	Θέλω ἕνα δωμάτιο γιά δύο ἤ τρεῖς μέρες/μία ἑβδομάδα/ὡς τή Παρασκευή thelo ena dhomatio ghia dhio i tris meres/mia evdhomadha/os ti paraskevi
What floor is the room on ?	Σέ ποιό πάτωμα εἶναι τό δωμάτιο; se pio patoma ine to dhomatio
Is there a lift/elevator?	Ἔχει ἀσανσέρ; ehi asanser
Have you a room on the first floor ?	Ἔχετε ἕνα δωμάτιο στό πρῶτο πάτωμα; ehete ena dhomatio sto proto patoma
May I see the room ?	Μπορῶ νά δῶ τό δωμάτιο; boro na dho to dhomatio
I like this room, I'll take it	Μ'ἀρέσει αὐτό τό δωμάτιο. Θά τό πάρω m'aressi afto to dhomatio; tha to paro
I don't like this room	Δέ μ'ἀρέσει αὐτό τό δωμάτιο dhe maressi afto to dhomatio

Have you another one?	Ἔχετε κανένα ἄλλο; ehete kanena alo
I want a quiet room	Θέλω ἕνα ἥσυχο δωμάτιο thelo ena issiho dhomatio
There's too much noise	Ἔχει πολύ θόρυβο ehi poli thorivo
I'd like a room with a balcony	Θά ἤθελα ἕνα δωμάτιο μέ μπαλκόνι tha ithela ena dhomatio me balkoni
Have you a room looking on to the street/sea?	Ἔχετε ἕνα δωμάτιο πού νά βλέπει στό δρόμο/στή θάλασσα; ehete ena dhomatio pou na vlepi sto dhromo/sti thalassa
We've only a double room	*Ἔχουμε μόνο διπλό δωμάτιο ehoume mono dhiplo dhomatio
This is the only room vacant	*Αὐτό εἶναι τό μόνο ἄδειο δωμάτιο afto ine to mono adhio dhomatio
We shall have another room tomorrow	*Θά ἔχουμε ἕνα ἄλλο δωμάτιο αὔριο tha ehoume ena alo dhomatio avrio

The room is only available tonight	*Τό δωμάτιο εἶναι ἐλεύθερο μόνον ἀπόψε to dhomatio ine elefthero mono apopse
How much is the room per night ?	Πόσο κάνει τό δωμάτιο τή νύχτα; posso kani to dhomatio ti nihta
Have you nothing cheaper ?	Δέν ἔχετε τίποτα πιό φθηνό; dhen ehete tipota pio fthino
Are service and tax included ?	Συμπεριλαμβάνεται ἡ ὑπηρεσία καί ὁ φόρος; simperilamvanete i ipiressia ke o foros
How much is the room without meals ?	Πόσο κάνει τό δωμάτιο χωρίς γεύματα; posso kani to dhomatio horis ghevmata
How much is full board/half board ?	Πόσο κάνει μέ ὅλα τά γεύματα/μόνο ἕνα; posso kani me ola ta ghevmata/mono ena
Is breakfast included in the price ?	Συμπεριλαμβάνεται τό πρόγευμα στή τιμή; simperilamvanete to proghevma sti timi

In your room

Could we have breakfast in our room, please?	Μπορούμε νά ἔχουμε πρόγευμα στό δωμάτιο μας παρακαλῶ; boroume na ehoume proghevma sto dhomatio mas parakalo
Please wake me at 8.30	Ξυπνῆστε με σᾶς παρακαλῶ στίς ὀκτώμιση xipniste me sas parakalo stis oktomissi
There's no ashtray in my room	Δέν ὑπάρχει σταχτοδοχεῖο στό δωμάτιο μου dhen iparhi stahtodhohio sto dhomatio mou
Can I have more hangers, please?	Μπορῶ νά ἔχω περισσότερες κρεμάστρες σᾶς παρακαλῶ; boro na eho perissoteres kremastres sas parakalo
Is there a point for an electric razor?	Ἔχει πρίζα γιά ἠλεκτρική ξυριστική μηχανή; ehi priza ghia ilektriki ksiristiki mihani
What's the voltage?[1]	Πόσα βόλτ εἶναι τό ρεῦμα; possa volt ine to revma

1. In Athens and most parts of the mainland the voltage is 220. On some of the islands it is 110 D.C.

Where is the bathroom/the lavatory?	Ποῦ εἶναι τό μπάνιο/τό ἀποχωρητήριο;
	pou ine to banio/to apohoritirio
Is there a shower?	Ἔχει ντούς;
	ehi douche
There are no towels in my room	Δέν ἔχει πετσέτες στό δωμάτιο μου
	dhen ehi petsetes sto dhomatio mou
There's no soap	Δέν ἔχει σαπούνι
	dhen ehi sapouni
There's no water	Δέν ἔχει νερό
	dhen ehi nero
There's no plug in my washbasin	Ὁ νυπτήρας μου δέν ἔχει βούλωμα
	o niptiras mou dhen ehi vouloma
There's no toilet paper in the lavatory	Δέν ἔχει χαρτί στό ἀποχωρητήριο
	dhen ehi harti sto apohoritirio
The lavatory won't flush	Δέν τρέχει τό νερό στό ἀποχωρητήριο
	dhen trehi to nero sto apohoritirio
May I have the key to the bathroom, please?	Μοῦ δίνετε τό κλειδί τοῦ μπάνιου παρακαλῶ;
	mou dhinete to klidhi tou baniou parakalo

May I have another blanket/ another pillow?	Μοῦ δίνετε ἄλλη μιά κουβέρτα/ ἄλλο ἕνα μαξιλλάρι mou dhinete ali mia kouverta/ alo ena maxilari
These sheets are dirty	Αὐτά τά σεντόνια εἶναι βρώμικα afta ta sendonia ine vromika
I can't open the window, please open it	Δέ μπορῶ ν'ἀνοίξω τό παράθυρο. Μοῦ τό ἀνοίγετε σᾶς παρακαλῶ dhen boro n'anixo to parathiro. mou t'anighete sas parakalo
It's too hot/cold	Κάνει πολύ ζέστη/κρύο kani poli zesti/krio
Can the heating be turned up/ turned down/turned off?	Μπορεῖτε νά ἀνεβάσετε/νά χαμηλώσετε/σβύσετε τή θέρμανση; borite n'anevassete/na hamilossete/na svissete ti thermanssi
Is the room air-conditioned?	Ἔχει τό δωμάτιο air condition; ehi to dhomatio air condition
The air conditioning doesn't work	Τό air condition δέν λειτουργεῖ to air condition dhen litourghi
Come in!	Ἐμπρός embros
Put it on the table, please	Ἀφίστετο στό τραπέζι παρακαλῶ afisteto sto trapezi parakalo

Would you clean these shoes, please ?	Μοῦ καθαρίζετε αὐτά τά παπούτσια παρακαλῶ; mou katharizete afta ta papoutsia parakalo
Would you clean this dress, please ?	Μοῦ καθαρίζετε αὐτό τό φόρεμα σᾶς παρακαλῶ; mou katharizete afto to forema sas parakalo
Would you press this suit, please ?	Μοῦ σιδερώνετε αὐτή τή φορεσιά παρακαλῶ; mou sidheronete afti ti foressia parakalo
When will it be ready ?	Πότε θά εἶναι ἕτοιμη; pote tha ine etimi
It will be ready tomorrow	*Θά εἶναι ἕτοιμη αὔριο tha ine etimi avrio

At the reception desk

Are there any letters for me ?	Ἔχω γράμματα; eho ghrammata
Are there any messages for me ?	Ἔχω τίποτα μηνύματα; eho tipota minimata

If anyone phones, tell them I'll be back at 4.30	*Ἄν τηλεφωνήσει κανείς, νά πεῖτε πώς θά ἐπιστρέψω στίς τεσσερισήμιση an tilefonissi kanis na pite pos tha epistrepso stis tesserissimissi
No one telephoned	*Δέν τηλεφώνησε κανείς dhen tilefonisse kanis
There's a lady/gentleman to see you	*Ἕνας κύριος/μία κυρία θέλει νά σᾶς δεῖ enas kirios/mia kiria theli na sas dhi
Please ask her/him to come up	Πέσ'τε της/του νά ἔρθει ἐπάνω pestetis/tou na erthi epano
I'm coming down	Κατεβαίνω kateveno
Have you any writing paper/ envelopes/stamps ?	Ἔχετε χαρτί ἐπιστολογραφίας/ φακέλλους/γραμματόσημα; ehete harti epistologhrafias/ fakelous/ghramatossima
Please send the chambermaid/the waiter	Στεῖλτε παρακαλῶ τήν καμαριέρα/τόν σερβιτόρο stilte paraklo tin kamariera/ton servitoro
I need a guide/an interpreter	Χρειάζομαι ἕναν ὁδηγό/ μεταφραστή hriazome enan odhigho/ metafrasti

Where is the dining room?	Ποῦ εἶναι ἡ τραπεζαρία; pou ine i trapezaria
What time is breakfast/lunch/dinner?	Τί ὥρα εἶναι τό πρόγευμα/μεσημεριανό/βραδυνό; ti ora ine to proghevma/messimeriano/vradhino
Is there a garage?	Ὑπάρχει γκαράζ; iparhi garaz
Is the hotel open all night?	Εἶναι ἀνοικτό τό ξενοδοχεῖο ὅλο τό βράδυ; ine anikto to xenodhohio olo to vradhi
What time does it close?	Τί ὥρα κλείνει; ti ora klini

Departure

I have to leave tomorrow	Πρέπει νά φύγω αὔριο prepi na figho avrio
Can you have my bill ready?	Μοῦ ἐτοιμάζετε τό λογαριασμό μου παρακαλῶ; mou etimazete to logharismo mou parakalo

I shall be coming back on . . .; can I book a room for that date ?	Θά ἐπιστρέψω στίς . . . Μπορῶ νά κλείσω ἕνα δωμάτιο γι'αὐτή τήν ἡμερομηνία;
	tha epistrepso stis . . . boro na klisso ena dhomatio ghiafti tin imerominia
Could you have my luggage brought down ?	Λέτε νά μοῦ φέρουν κάτω τίς ἀποσκευές μου;
	lete na mou feroun kato tis aposkeves mou
Please call a taxi for me	Φωνάξτε ἕνα ταξί σᾶς παρακαλῶ
	fonaxte ena taxi sas parakalo
Thank you for a pleasant stay	Εὐχαριστῶ γιά τήν εὐχάριστη διαμονή
	efharisto ghia tin efharisti dhiamoni

RESTAURANT

Going to a restaurant

Can you suggest a good cheap restaurant ?	Μπορεῖτε νά μοῦ συστήσετε ἕνα καλό φθηνό ἐστιατόριο;
	borite na mou sistissete ena kalo fthino estiatorio
I'd like to book a table for four at 1 p.m.	Θέλω νά κλείσω ἕνα τραπέζι γιά τέσσερις στίς μία ἡ ὥρα
	thelo na klisso ena trapezi ghia tesseris stis mia i ora
I've reserved a table; my name is . . .	Ἔχω κλείσει τραπέζι. Λέγομαι...
	eho klissi trapezi. leghome
Have you a table for three ?	Ἔχετε ἕνα τραπέζι γιά τρεῖς;
	ehete ena trapezi ghia tris
Is there a table free on the terrace ?	Ὑπάρχει κανένα ἐλεύθερο τραπέζι στήν ταράτσα;
	iparhi kanena elefthero trapezi stin taratsa
We shall have a table free in half an hour	*Θά ἔχουμε ἕνα τραπέζι σέ μισή ὥρα
	tha ehoume ena trapezi se missi ora

We don't serve lunch until 12.30	*Δέν σερβίρουμε μεσημεριανό πρίν ἀπ'τίς δωδεκάμιση dhen serviroume messimeriano prin aptis dhodhekamissi
We don't serve dinner until 8 o'clock	*Δέν σερβίρουμε βραδυνό πρίν ἀπ'τίς ὀκτώ dhen serviroume vradhino prin aptis okto
We stop serving at 11 o'clock	*Δέν σερβίρουμε μετά ἀπ'τίς ἕντεκα dhen serviroume meta aptis endeka
Where is the cloakroom?	Ποῦ εἶναι ἡ γκαρνταρόμπα; pou ine i gardaroba
It is downstairs	*Εἶναι κάτω ine kato
We are in a hurry	Βιαζόμαστε viazomaste
Do you serve snacks?	Ἔχετε μεζέδες; ehete mezedhes
That was an excellent meal	Περίφημο γεῦμα perifimo ghevma
We shall come again	Θά ξανάρθουμε tha ksanarthoume

Ordering

Service charge	*Ποσοστά σερβιτόρου possosta servitorou
Cover charge	*Κουβέρ kouver
Waiter/waitress	Σερβιτόρος/σερβιτόρα servitoros/servitora
May I see the menu/the wine list, please?	Μπορῶ νά δῶ τό menu παρακαλῶ/τήν λίστα κρασιῶν; boro na dho to menu parakalo/ti lista krassion
Is there a set menu for lunch?	Εἶναι τό μεσημεριανό φαγητό ταμπλ-ντότ; ine to messimeriano faghito table d' hôte
What do you recommend?	Τί μοῦ συστήνετε; ti mou sistinete
Can you tell me what this is?	Τί εἶναι αὐτό; ti ine afto
What are the specialities of the restaurant/of the region?	Ποιές εἶναι οἱ σπεσιαλιτέ σας/τῆς περιοχῆς; pies ine i spessialite sas/tis periohis

Would you like to try . . . ?	*Θέλετε νά δοκιμάσετε . . .; thelete na dhokimassete
There's no more . . .	*Τέλειωσε τό . . . teliosse to
I'd like . . .	Θά ἤθελα . . . tha ithela
Is it hot or cold ?	Εἶναι ζεστό ἤ κρύο; ine zesto i krio;
This isn't what I ordered, I want . . .	Δέν παράγγειλα αὐτό. Θέλω . . . dhen parangila afto. thelo
I don't want any oil/sauce with it	Δέ θέλω λάδι/σάλτσα dhen thelo ladhi/saltsa
Some more bread, please	Λίγο ἀκόμα ψωμί παρακαλῶ ligho akoma psomi parakalo
A little more, please	Λίγο ἀκόμα παρακαλῶ ligho akoma parakalo
This is bad/uncooked/stale	Αὐτό εἶναι χαλασμένο/ἄψητο/ μπαγιάτικο afto ino halasmeno/apsito/ baghiatiko

Drinks

What will you have to drink ?	*Τί θά πιεῖτε; ti tha piite
A bottle of the local wine, please	Ένα μπουκάλι ντόπιο κρασί παρακαλῶ ena boukali dopio krassi parakalo
Do you serve wine by the glass ?	Σερβίρετε κρασί μέ τό ποτήρι; servirete krassi me to potiri
Two glasses of beer, please	Δύο ποτήρια μπύρα παρακαλῶ dhio potiria bira parakalo
Two more beers	Δύο ἀκόμα μπύρες dhio akoma bires
I'd like another glass of water, please	Άλλο ἕνα ποτήρι νερό παρακαλῶ alo ena potiri nero parakalo
The same again, please	Ξανά τό ἴδιο παρακαλῶ ksana to idhio parakalo
Three black coffees and one with cream	Τρεῖς nescafé χωρίς γάλα κι ἕνα μέ γάλα tris nescafé horis ghala kiena me ghala

Turkish coffee (bitter, medium, sweet)

Τούρκικο καφέ (πικρό, μέτριο, γλυκό)
tourkiko kafe (pikro, metrio, ghliko)

May we have an ashtray?

Ένα σταχτοδοχείο παρακαλώ;
ena stahtodhohio parakalo

Can I have a light, please?

Έχετε φωτιά παρακαλώ;
ehete fotia parakalo

Paying

The bill, please

Παρακαλώ τό λογαριασμό
parakalo to loghariasmo

Does it include service?

Συμπεριλαμβάνει τό σερβίς;
simberilamvani to servis

Please check the bill – I don't think it's correct

Ξανακάντε τό λογαριασμό σᾶς παρακαλώ—νομίζω ὅτι εἶναι λάθος
ksanakante to loghariasmo sas parakalo—nomizo oti ine lathos

I didn't have soup

Δέν πῆρα σούπα
dhen pira soupa

I had chicken, not steak

Πῆρα κοτόπουλο, ὅχι μπιφτέκι
pira kotopouio, oni bifteki

May we have separate bills?

Μπορούμε νά 'χουμε ξεχωρι-
στούς λογαριασμούς;
boroume nahoume xehoristous
loghariasmous

Breakfast

What time is breakfast served?

Τί ὥρα σερβίρετε τό πρόγευμα;
ti ora servirete to proghevma

A large white coffee, please

Ἕνα nescafé μέ γάλα παρακαλῶ
ena nescafé me ghala parakalo

A black coffee

Ἕνα nescafé χωρίς γάλα
ena nescafé horis ghala

A cup of tea, please

Ἕνα φλιτζάνι τσάϊ παρακαλῶ
ena fliidzani tsai parakalo

I'd like tea with milk/lemon

Θέλω τσάϊ μέ γάλα/λεμόνι
thelo tsai me ghala/lemoni

May we have some sugar, please?

Λίγη ζάχαρη παρακαλῶ
lighi zahari parakalo

A roll and butter

ἕνα ψωμάκι καί βούτυρο
ena psomaki ke voutiro

Toast

Φρηγανιά
frighania

We'd like more butter, please	Λίγο ἀκόμα βούτυρο παρακαλῶ **ligho akoma voutiro parakalo**
Have you some jam/marmalade ?	Ἔχετε λίγη μαρμελάδα; **ehete lighi marmeladha**
I would like a hard-boiled egg/ soft-boiled egg	Θέλω ἕνα σφιχτό/νερουλό αὐγό **thelo ena sfihto/neroulo avgho**
What fruit juices do you have ?	Τί χυμούς φρούτων ἔχετε; **ti himous frouton ehete**

Restaurant vocabulary

---

ashtray	σταχτοδοχεῖο **stahtodhohio**
bar	bar
beer	μπύρα **bira**
bill	λογαριασμός **loghariasmos**
bottle/half bottle	μπουκάλι/μισό μπουκάλι **boukali/misso boukali**
bowl	bowl
bread	ψωμί **psomi**

butter	βούτυρο **voutiro**
carafe	καράφα **karafa**
cigarettes	τσιγάρα **tsighara**
cloakroom	γκαρνταρόμπα **gardaroba**
coffee	καφές **kafes**
course (dish)	πιάτο **piato**
cream	κρέμα **krema**
cup	φλιτζάνι **flidzani**
fork	πειρούνι **pirouni**
glass	ποτήρι **potiri**
hungry (to be)	πεινάω **pinao**
knife	μαχαίρι **maheri**
lemon	λεμόνι **lemoni**

matches	σπίρτα
	spirta
mayonnaise	μαγιονέζα
	maghioneza
menu	menu *or* κατάλογος
	kataloghos
milk	γάλα
	ghala
mustard	μουστάρδα
	moustardha
napkin	πετσέτα
	petseta
oil	λάδι
	ladhi
pepper	πιπέρι
	piperi
plate	πιάτο
	piato
restaurant	ἑστιατόριο
	estiatorio
salt	ἁλάτι
	alati
sandwich	sandwich
sauce	σάλτσα
	saltsa

saucer	πιατάκι **piataki**
service	υπηρεσία **ipiressia**
snack	μεζές **mezes**
spoon	κουτάλι **koutali**
sugar	ζάχαρη **zahari**
table	τραπέζι **trapezi**
tablecloth	τραπεζομάντηλο **trapezomantilo**
tea	τσάι **tsai**
terrace	ταράτσα **taratsa**
thirsty (to be)	δειψάω **dhipsao**
tip	πουρμπουάρ **pourbouar**
toothpick	οδοντογλυφίδα **odhontoghlifidha**
vegetarian	χορτοφάγος **hortofaghos**

vinegar	ξύδι **xidhi**
waiter	σερβιτόρος **servitoros**
waitress	σερβιτόρα **servitora**
water	νερό **nero**
wine	κρασί **krassi**
wine list	κατάλογος κρασιῶν **kataloghos krassion**

MENU

ΣΟΥΠΕΣ	soupes	SOUPS
κονσομέ	consommé	consommé
σούπα φασόλια	soupa fassolia	bean soup
σούπα φακές	soupa fakies	lentil soup
ντοματόσουπα	domatossoupa	tomato soup
σούπα λαχανικῶν	soupa lahanikon	vegetable soup
φιδέ	fidhes	vermicelli soup
κοτόσουπα	kotossoupa	chicken soup
ψαρόσουπα	psarossoupa	fish soup
αὐγολέμονο	avgholemono	egg and lemon soup
τραχανάς	trahanas	pasta soup

ΟΡΕΚΤΙΚΑ ΚΑΙ ΠΡΩΤΑ	orektika ke prota	HORS D'ŒUVRES AND FIRST COURSES
καλαμαράκια	kalamarakia	fried baby squid
μαρίδες	maridhes	whitebait
σκορδαλιά	skordhalia	garlic dip
ταραμοσαλάτα	taramossalata	cod roe salad
μελιτζανοσαλάτα	melidzanossalata	aubergine salad
σαχανάκι	sahanaki	fried cheese
ἐλιές	elies	olives
θαλασσινά	thalassina	shellfish, sea food

γεμιστές ντομάτες	ghemistes domates	stuffed tomatoes
γεμιστές πιπεριές	ghemistes piperies	stuffed peppers
γεμιστές μελιτζάνες	ghemistes melidzanes	stuffed aubergines
ἀγκινάρες ἀλά πολίτα	anginares ala polita	artichokes cooked in olive oil, with onions and potatoes
φασολάκια πλακί	fassolakia plaki	dried beans cooked in olive oil and tomatoes
ντολμάδες, ντολμαδάκια	dolmadhes, dolmadhakia	stuffed cabbage leaves (or vine leaves)
αὐγοτάραχο	avghotaraho	dry cod roe
ταραμάς	taramas	cod roe
μπρίκ	brik	red caviar
χαβιάρι	mavro haviari	black caviar
ZYMAPIKA	zimarika	PASTA
μακαρόνια	makaronia	spaghetti
παστίτσιο	pastitsio	baked macaroni
κριθαράκι	kritharaki	rice-shaped pasta
χυλοπίτες	hilopites	short noodles
PIZI	pizi	RICE
πιλάφι	pilafi	rice pilaf
πιλάφι μέ μπιζελάκια	pilafi me bizelakia	rice with peas

πιλάφι μέ μήδεια	pilafi me midhia	rice with mussels
πιλάφι μέ γιαούρτι	pilafi me ghiaourti	rice with yoghurt
πιλάφι μέ σηκωτάκια	pilafi me sikotakia	rice with liver
σπανακόριζο	spanakorizo	rice with spinach
ΨΑΡΙΑ	psari	FISH
ἀστακός	astakos	lobster
λυθρίνι	lithrini	bream
μπαρμπούνι	barbouni	red mullet
καλαμάρια	kalamaria	squid
ξιφιός	xifios	sword fish
συναγρίδα	sinaghridha	red snapper
μαρίδες	maridhes	whitebait
μπακαλιάρος	bakaliaros	cod (usually dry salted)
ὀκταπόδι	oktapodhi	octopus
ψάρι σχάρας	psari skharas	grilled fish
ψητό ψάρι	psito psari	baked fish
τηγανιτά ψάρια	tighanita psaria	fried fish
ἀχινοί	ahini	sea urchins
σολομός	solomos	salmon
σαρδέλες	sardheles	sardines
γλῶσσα	ghlossa	sole
σουπιές	soupies	ink fish

| τσιποῦρα | tsipoura | bream |
| κέφαλος | kefalos | mullet |

ΚΡΕΑΣ	kreas	MEAT
ἀρνί	arni	lamb
ψητό	psito	roast
ψητό χειρινοῦ	psito hirinou	roast pork
μπιφτέκι	bifteki	steak
μπριζόλα	brizola	chop
βραστό βοδινό	vrasto vodhino	boiled beef
μυαλά	miala	brains
ψητό μοσχαράκι	psito mosharaki	roast veal
σηκώτι	sikoti	liver
γλῶσσα	ghlossa	tongue
μοσχαρίσιες μπριζόλες	mosharissies brizoles	veal chops
χοιρινές μπριζόλες	hirines brizoles	pork chops
ἀρνίσιες μπριζόλες	arnissies brizoles	lamb chops
παϊδάκια	paidhakia	lamb cutlets
κεφτέδες	keftedhes	meat balls
νεφρά	nefra	kidneys
λουκάνικα	loukanika	sausages
μουσακάς	moussakas	moussaka

φιλέτο σχάρας	fileto skharas	grilled steak
κοκορέτσι	kokoretsi	lamb innards on the spit (intestines, liver, spleen, kidneys, heart)
ἀρνάκι σούβλας	arnaki souvlas	lamb on the spit
σουβλάκια	souvlakia	kebab
ΠΟΥΛΕΡΙΚΑ	poulerika	POULTRY
χήνα	hina	goose
φασιανός	fassianos	pheasant
γαλοπούλα	ghalopoula	turkey
κοτόπουλο	kotopoulo	chicken
πόδι κότας	podhi kotas	leg of chicken
στῆθος κότας	stithos kotas	chicken breast
ΛΑΧΑΝΙΚΑ ΚΑΙ ΣΑΛΑΤΕΣ	lahanika ke soupes	VEGETABLES AND SALADS
σκόρδο	skordho	garlic
σπαράγκια	sparagia	asparagus
παντζάρια	pandzaria	beetroots
ἀγκινάρες	anginares	artichokes
καρότα	karota	carrots
κουνουπίδι	kounoupidhi	cauliflower

λάχανο	lahano	cabbage
μπιζέλια	bizelia	peas
ἀγγούρι	angouri	cucumber
κρεμμύδι	kremidhi	onion
φρέσκα φασολάκια	freska fassolakia	green beans
γίγαντες	ghighantes	broad beans
μανιτάρια	manitaria	mushrooms
μαρούλι	marouli	lettuce
μελιτζάνες	melidzanes	aubergine
πατάτες	patates	potatoes
ντομάτες	domates	tomatoes
πιπεριές	piperies	peppers
πράσα	prassa	leeks
ρεπανάκια	rapanakia	radishes
μαϊντανός	maïdanos	parsley
σέλινο	selino	celery
σπανάκι	spanaki	spinach
κολοκυθάκια	kolokithakia	courgettes
ραδίκια	radhikia	dandelions
μπάμιες	bamies	okra
κουκκιά	koukia	fava beans
καλαμπόκι	kalamboki	corn

ΤΥΡΙΑ	tyria	CHEESE
φέτα	feta	(white, sharp and salty, often made of lamb's or goat's milk)
κασέρι	kasseri	(the nearest to Cheddar, but made of lamb's milk and smoother and richer)
μανοῦρι	manouri	(white, almost no salt added, very creamy)
κεφαλοτύρι	kefalotiri	(very salty version of kasseri, almost like Parmesan)
ροκφόρ	rokfor	blue cheese
ΑΥΓΑ	avgha	EGGS
αὐγά τηγανιτά—μάτια	avgha tighanita, matia	fried eggs
ὀμελέτα	omeleta	omelette
βραστά αὐγά	vrasta avgha	boiled eggs
ΓΛΥΚΙΣΜΑΤΑ	ghliki smata	DESSERTS
παγωτό	paghoto	ice cream
τούρτα	tourta	trifle
κέϊκ	cake	cake/gâteau

φρουτοσαλάτα	froutosalata	fruit salad
πάστες	pastes	pastry
κρέμα	krema	pudding
κρέμ καραμέλ	krem karamel	cream caramel
κομπόστα	komposta	compôte
μπακλαβάς	baklava	very fine crispy pastry with nuts and syrup or honey
καταΐφι	kataifi	fine shredded pastry with nuts and syrup or honey
γαλακτομπούρεκο	ghalaktoboureko	very fine crispy pastry with custard and syrup
λουκούμι	loukoumi	Turkish delight
γιαούρτι	ghiaourti	yogurt
ΦΡΟΥΤΑ ΚΑΙ ΞΕΡΟΙ ΚΑΡΠΟΙ	frouta ke kseri karpi	FRUIT AND NUTS
βερύκοκα	verikoka	apricots
ροδάκινα	rodhakina	peaches
πορτοκάλι	portokali	orange
σταφύλια	stafilia	grapes
πεπόνι	peponi	melon
καρπούζι	karpouzi	water melon

μπανάνα	banana	banana
κεράσια	kerassia	cherries
μούσμουλα	mousmoula	medlars
σῦκα	sika	figs
δαμάσκηνα	dhamaskina	prunes
φράουλες	fraoules	strawberries
μοῦρα	moura	mulberries
ἀμύγδαλα	amighdhala	almonds
καρύδια	karidhia	walnuts
σταφίδες	stafidhes	raisins
μῆλο	milo	apple
ἀχλάδι	ahladhi	pear
φυστίκια	fistikia	pistachios

ΤΡΟΠΟΙ ΜΑΓΕΙΡΕΜΑΤΟΣ	tropi mayhirematos	WAYS OF COOKING
καπνιστό	kapnisto	smoked
μέ βούτυρο	me voutiro	with butter
μέ λάδι – λαδερό	me ladhi *or* ladhero	with olive oil
ψητό	psito	roast *or* baked
κοκκινιστό	kokinisto	cooked with butter and tomatoes
σχάρας	skharas	grilled
τηγανιτό	tighanito	fried

καλοψημένο	kalopsimeno	well done
άψητο	apsito	underdone
ωμό	omo	raw
βραστό	vrasto	boiled
γεμιστό	ghemisto	stuffed
ΠΟΤΑ	pota	DRINKS
μεταλλικό νερό	metaliko nero	mineral water
πορτοκαλάδα	portokaladha	orangade
λεμονάδα	lemonadha	lemonade (made with lemon juice)
γκαζόζα	gazoza	lemonade
μπύρα	bira	beer
κονιάκ	koniak	cognac
κρασί μπρούσκο	krassi brousko	dry red wine
κρασί άσπρο	krassi aspro	white wine
ρετσίνα	retsina	resinated white wine

SHOPPING[1]

Where to go

Where are the best department stores ?	Ποῦ εἶναι τά καλύτερα καταστήματα; pou ine ta kalitera **katastimata**
Where is the market ?	Ποῦ εἶναι ἡ ἀγορά; pou **ine** i aghora
Is there a market every day ?	Εἶναι ἀνοικτή ἡ ἀγορά κάθε μέρα; ine **anikti** i aghora kathe mera
Where's the nearest chemist ?	Ποῦ εἶναι τό πλησιέστερο φαρμακεῖο; pou ine to plissiestero **farmakio**
Can you recommend a barber/ hairdresser ?	Μπορεῖτε νά μοῦ συστήσετε ἕνα κουρέα/κομμωτήριο; borite na mou sistissete ena kourea/komotirio
Baker	(Ἀρτοποιεῖον) Ψωμᾶς (artopiion) psomas
Butcher	Χασάπης hasapis

1. Shopping hours are 8.30 to 13.45 and 17.00 to 20.00 from May to October, and 8.30 to 13.15 and 16.00 to 19.30 the rest of the year.

Chemist	(person) Φαρμακοποιός
	(shop) Φαρμακεῖο
	farmakopios/farmakio
Dairy	Γαλακτοπωλεῖον
	ghalaktopolion
Dry cleaner's	Καθαριστήριο
	katharistirio
Grocer	Μπακάλης (Μπακάλικο)
	bakalis (bakaliko)
Greengrocer	Μανάβης (Μανάβικο)
	manavis (manaviko)
Laundry	Πλυντήριο
	plintirio
Newsagent	Ἐφημεριδοπώλης
	efimeridhopolis
Stationer	Χαρτοπωλεῖον
	hartopolion
Tobacconist	Καπνοπωλεῖο
	kapnopolio
Where can I buy ...?	Ποῦ μπορῶ ν'ἀγοράσω ...
	pou boro n'aghorasso
When do the shops open/close?	Πότε ἀνοίγουν/κλείνουν τά καταστήματα
	pote anighoun klinoun ta katastimata

In the shop

Sale (clearance)	*Ξεπούλημα xepoulima
Cash desk	*Ταμείο tamio
Shop assistant	Βοηθός voïthos
Manager	Διευθυντής dhiefthindis
Can I help you?	*Μπορῶ νά σᾶς βοηθήσω; boro na sas voïthisso
I want to buy ...	Θέλω ν'ἀγοράσω ... thelo n'aghorasso
Do you sell ...?	Πουλᾶτε ...; poulate
I just want to look around	Θέλω μόνο νά κοιτάξω thelo mono na kitaxo
I don't want to buy anything now	Δέν θέλω ν'ἀγοράσω τίποτα τώρα dhen thelo n'aghorasso tipota tora

We've sold out but we'll have more tomorrow	*Δέν ἔχουμε ἄλλο, ἀλλά ἐλᾶτε αὔριο πάλι dhen ehoume alo, ala elate avrio pali
Will you take it with you?	*Θά τό πάρετε μαζί σας; tha to parete mazi sas
Please send them to this address/this hotel	*Σᾶς παρακαλῶ στεῖλτε τα σ'αὐτή τή διεύθυνση/σ'αὐτό τό ξενοδοχεῖο sas parakalo stilteta safti ti dhiefthinssi/safto to xenodhohio

Choosing

What colour do you want?	*Τί χρῶμα θέλετε; ti hroma thelete
I like this one	Μ'άρέσει αὐτό m'aressi afto
I prefer that one	Προτιμῶ αὐτό protimo afto
I don't like this colour	Δέ μ'άρέσει αὐτό τό χρῶμα dhe m'aressi afto to hroma

Have you a green one?	Ἔχετε ἕνα πράσινο; ehete ena prassino
Do you have one in a different colour?	Ἔχετε κανένα ἄλλο χρῶμα; ehete kanena alo hroma
Have you anything better?	Ἔχετε τίποτα καλύτερο; ehete tipota kalitero
I'd like another	Θά 'θελα ἕνα ἄλλο tha'thela ena alo
What size?[1]	Τί μέγεθος; ti meghethos
It's too big/tight	Εἶναι πολύ μεγάλο/στενό ine poli meghalo/steno
Have you a larger/smaller one?	Ἔχετε ἕνα μεγαλύτερο/ μικρότερο; ehete ena meghalitero/ mikrotero
What size is this?	Τί μέγεθος εἶναι αὐτό; ti meghethos ine afto
I want size ...	Θέλω μέγεθος ... thelo meghethos
The English/American size is ...	Τό Ἐγγλέζικο/Ἀμερικάνικο μέγεθος εἶναι ... to engl">eziko/amerikaniko meghethos ine

1. See p. 120 for table of continental sizes.

My collar size is . . .	Τό μέγεθος τοῦ κολλάρου μου εἶναι . . . to meghethos tou kolarou mou **ine**
My chest measurement is . . .	Τό μέγεθος τοῦ στήθους μου εἶναι . . . to meghethos tou stithous mou **ine**
My waist measurement is . . .	Ἡ μέση μου εἶναι . . . i messi mou **ine**
What's it made of?	Ἀπό τί εἶναι; apo ti **ine**

Complaints

I want to see the manager	Θέλω νά δῶ τόν διευθυντή thelo na dho ton dhiefthindi
I bought this yesterday	Τ'ἀγόρασα χθές t'aghorassa hthes
It doesn't work	Δέν λειτουργεῖ dhen litourghi

This is dirty/stained/torn/broken/ cracked	Αὐτό εἶναι βρώμικο/ λεκιασμένο/σκισμένο/ σπασμένο/ραγισμένο
	afto ine vromiko/lekiasmeno/ skizmeno/spasmeno/ raghismeno
Will you change it please?	Μοῦ τ'ἀλλάζετε παρακαλῶ; mou t'alazete parakalo
Will you refund my money?	Θά μοῦ ἐπιστρέψετε τά χρήματα μου; tha mou epistrepsete ta hrimata mou

Paying

How much is this?	Πόσο κάνει αὐτό; posso kani afto
That's . . . please	*Αὐτό εἶναι . . . παρακαλῶ afto ine . . . parakalo
They are . . . each	*Αὐτά κάνουν . . . τό ἕνα afta kanoun . . . to ena
It's too expensive	Εἶναι πολύ ἀκριβό ine poli akrivo
Don't you have anything cheaper?	Δέν ἔχετε τίποτα φθηνότερο; dhen ehete tipota fthinotero

Will you take English/American currency ?	Παίρνετε 'Αγγλικα/ 'Αμερικάνικα χρήματα; pernete anglika/amerikanika hrimata
Do you take travellers' cheques ?	Παίρνετε travellers' cheques; pernete travellers' cheques
Please pay the cashier	Πληρῶστε στό ταμεῖο παρακαλῶ pliroste sto tamio parakalo
May I have a receipt, please ?	Μοῦ δίνετε μία ἀπόδειξη παρακαλῶ; mou dhinete mia apodhixi parakalo
You've given me too little/ too much change	Μοῦ δώσατε λιγότερα/ περισσότερα ρέστα mou dhossate lighotera/ perissotera resta

Clothes and shoes[1]

I want a hat/sunhat	Θέλω ἕνα καπέλλο/ καπέλλο γιά τόν ἥλιο thelo ena kapelo/ kapelo ghia ton ilio

1. For sizes see p. 120

I'd like a pair of gloves

Θέλω ἕνα ζευγάρι γάντια
thelo ena zevghari ghantia

Can I look at dresses, please?

Μπορῶ νά δῶ μερικά φορέματα
παρακαλῶ;
boro na dho merika foremata
parakalo

I like the one in the window

Μ᾽ἀρέσει αὐτό πού εἶναι στή
βιτρίνα
m'aressi afto pou ine sti
vitrina

May I try this?

Μπορῶ νά δοκιμάσω αὐτό;
boro na dhokimasso afto

That's smart

Αὐτό εἶναι κομψό
afto ine kompso

It doesn't fit me

Δέ μοῦ 'ρχετε καλά
dhe mou'rhete kala

I don't like the style

Δέ μ᾽ἀρέσει τό στύλ
dhe m'aressi to stil

Where's the coat department?

Ποῦ εἶναι τά παλτά;
pou ine ta palta

Where are beach clothes?

Ποῦ εἶναι τά ροῦχα γιά τήν
πλάζ;
pou ine ta rouha ghia tin
plaz

The men's department is on the
second floor

*Τό τμῆμα ἀνδρικῶν ρούχων
εἶναι στό δεύτερο πάτωμα
to tmima andhrikon rouhon
ine sto dheftero patoma

I want a short/long sleeved shirt, collar size . . .	Θέλω ἕνα πουκάμισο μέ κοντά/ μακρυά μανίκια μέγεθος . . . thelo ena poukamisso me konta/makria manikia meghethos
A pair of grey wool socks, please, size . . .	Ἕνα ζευγάρι γκρίζες μάλλινες κάλτσες, μέγεθος . . . ena zevghari grizes malines kaltses meghethos
I need a pair of walking shoes	Χρειάζομαι ἕνα ζευγάρι παπούτσια γιά περπάτημα hriazome ena zevghari papoutsia ghia perpatima
I need a pair of beach sandals/ black shoes	Χρειάζομαι ἕνα ξευγάρι σανδάλια/μαῦρα παπούτσια hriazome ena zevghari sandhalia/mavra papoutsia
These heels are too high/too low	Αὐτά τά τακούνια εἶναι πολύ ψηλά/χαμηλα afta ta takounia ine poli psila/hamila

Clothing sizes

WOMEN'S DRESSES, ETC.

British	32	34	36	38	40	42	44
American	10	12	14	16	18	20	22
Continental	30	32	34	36	38	40	42

MEN'S SUITS

British and American	36	38	40	42	44	46
Continental	46	48	50	52	54	56

MEN'S SHIRTS

British and American	14	14½	15	15½	16	16½	17
Continental	36	37	38	39	41	42	43

STOCKINGS

British and American	8	8½	9	9½	10	10½	11
Continental	0	1	2	3	4	5	6

SOCKS

British and American	9½	10	10½	1	11½
Continental	38–39	39–40	40–41	41–42	42–43

SHOES

British	1	2	3	4	5	6		7	8	9	10	11	12
American	2½	3½	4½	5½	6½	7½		8½	9½	10½	11½	12½	13½
Continental	33	34–5	36	37	38	39–40		41	42	43	44	45	46

This table is only intended as a rough guide since sizes vary from manufacturer to manufacturer.

Chemist[1]

Can you prepare this prescription for me, please?	Μοῦ ἑτοιμάζετε αὐτή τή συνταγή παρακαλῶ; mou etimazete afti ti sintaghi parakalo
Have you a small first aid kit?	Ἔχετε ἕνα μικρό κουτί μέ πρῶτες βοήθειες; ehete ena mikro kouti me protes voithies
A bottle of aspirin, please	Ἕνα μπουκάλι ἀσπιρίνες παρακαλῶ ena boukali aspirines parakalo
A tin of adhesive plaster	Λευκοπλάστη lefkoplasti

1. See also AT THE DOCTOR'S (p. 154)

Can you suggest something for indigestion/constipation/ diarrhoea ?	Τί θά μοῦ συστήνατε γιά δυσπεψία/δυσκοιλιότητα/ διάρρεια ti tha mou sistinate ghia dhispepsia/dhiskiliotita/ dhiaria
I want something for insect bites	Θέλω κάτι γιά τσιμπήματα ἀπό ἔντομα thelo kati ghia tsimbimata apo entoma
Can you give me something for sunburn ?	Μοῦ δίνετε κάτι γιά κάψιμο ἀπό τόν ἥλιο; mou dhinete kati ghia kapsimo apo ton ilio
I want some throat/cough lozenges	Θέλω κάτι γιά τό λαιμό μου/ γιά τό βῆχα thelo kati ghia ton lemo mou/ ghia ton viha

Toilet requisites

A packet of razor blades, please	Ἕνα κουτάκι μέ ξυράφια παρακαλῶ ena koutaki me xirafia parakalo

Have you an after-shave lotion?	Ἔχετε καμιά λοσιόν γιά μετά τό ξύρισμα; ehete kamia lossion ghia meta to xirisma
How much is this lotion?	Πόσο κάνει αὐτή ἡ λοσιόν; posso kani afti i lossion
A tube of toothpaste, please	Μία ὀδοντόπαστα παρακαλῶ mia odhontopasta parakalo
Give me a box of paper handkerchiefs, please	Ἕνα κουτί μέ χαρτομάντηλα παρακαλῶ ena kouti me hartomandila parakalo
I want some eau-de-cologne/perfume	Θέλω λίγη κολώνια/ἄρωμα thelo lighi kolonia/aroma
What kinds of soap have you?	Τί σαπούνια ἔχετε; ti sapounia ehete
A bottle/tube of shampoo, please, for dry/greasy hair	Ἕνα μπουκάλι/σωληνάριο σαμπού παρακαλῶ γιά ξερά/λιπαρά μαλλιά ena boukali/solinario shampoo parakalo ghia xera/lipara malia

Photography

I want to buy a (cine) camera	Θέλω ν'ἀγοράσω μία (κινηματογραφική) μηχανή thelo n'aghorasso mia (kinimatoghrafiki) mihani
Have you a film for this camera ?	Ἔχετε φίλμ γι'αὐτή τή μηχανή; ehete film ghiafti ti mihani
Can I have a 33 mm. colour film with 20/36 exposures ?	Μπορῶ νά ἔχω ἕνα φίλμ τῶν τριανταπέντε μιλιμέτρ, ἔγχρωμο γιά εἴκοσι/τριανταέξη ἐμφανίσεις; boro na eho ena film ton triantapende milimetre, enhromo ghia ikossi/triantaexi emfanissis
Would you fit the film in the camera for me, please ?	Μοῦ βάζετε τό φίλμ στή μηχανή μου σᾶς παρακαλῶ; mou vazete to film sti mihani mou sas parakalo
How much is it ?	Πόσο κάνει; posso kani
Does the price include processing ?	Συμπεριλαμβάνεται ἡ ἐμφάνιση στή τιμή; simberilamvanete i emfanissi sti timi

I'd like this film developed and
printed

Θέλω νά μοῦ ἐμφανίσετε αὐτό
   τό φίλμ
thelo na mou emfanissete afto
   to film

Please enlarge this negative

Μοῦ μεγεθύνετε σᾶς παρακαλῶ
   αὐτό τό ἀρνητικό
mou meghethinete sas parakalo
   afto to arnitiko

When will they be ready?

Πότε θά εἶναι ἔτοιμες;
pote tha ine etimes

Will they be done tomorrow?

Θά'ναι ἔτοιμες αὔριο;
tha'ne etimes avrio

My camera's not working, can you
mend it?

Ἡ μηχανή μου δέ λειτουργεῖ.
   Μπορεῖτε νά μοῦ τήν
   ἐπιδιορθώσετε;
i mihani mou dhe litourghi.
   borite na mou tin
   epidhiorthossete

The film is jammed

Ἔχει πιάσει τό φίλμ
ehi piassi to film

Lens

Φακός
fakos

Lightmeter

Φωτόμετρο
fotometro

Food[1]

Give me a kilo/ half a kilo of . . ., please	Δῶστε μου ἕνα κιλό/μισό κιλό . . . παρακαλῶ **dhoste mou ena kilo/misso kilo . . . parakalo**
I want some sweets/chocolate	Θέλω λίγα γλυκά/σοκολάτα **thelo ligha ghiika/sokolata**
A bottle of milk	Ἕνα μπουκάλι γάλα **ena boukali ghala**
Is there anything back on the bottle ?	Ἐπιστρέφεται τίποτα γιά τό μπουκάλι; **epistrefete tipota ghia to boukali**
A kilo/half a kilo of wine	Ἕνα κιλό/μισό κιλό κρασί **ena kilo/misso kilo krassi**
A bottle of beer	Ἕνα μπουκάλι μπύρα **ena boukali bira**
I want a jar/tin/packet of . . .	Θέλω ἕνα βάζο/μία κονσέρβα/ἕνα πακέτο . . . **thelo ena vazo/mia konsserva/ena paketo**

1. See also RESTAURANT (p. 88) and WEIGHTS AND MEASURES (p. 177).

Do you sell frozen foods ?	Πουλᾶτε κατεψυγμένα τρόφιμα/; poulate katepsighmena trofima
These pears are too hard	Αὐτά τ'ἀχλάδια εἶναι πολύ σκληρά afta t'ahladhia ine poli sklira
Is it fresh ?	Εἶναι φρέσκο; ine fresko
Are they ripe ?	Εἶναι γινομένα; ine ghinomena
This is bad/stale	Εἶναι χαλασμένο/μπαγιάτικο ine halasmeno/baghiatiko
A loaf of bread	Μία φραντζόλα ψωμί mia frandzola psomi
How much a kilo	Πόσο τό κιλό; posso to kilo

Tobacconist

Do you stock English/American cigarettes ?	Ἔχετε Ἀγγλικά/Ἀμερικανικά τσιγάρα; ehete anglika/amerikanika tsighara

What English cigarettes have you ?	Τί 'Αγγλικά τσιγάρα ἔχετε; ti anglika tsighara ehete
A packet of ...	Ἔνα κουτί ... ena kouti
I want some filter tip cigarettes/ cigarettes without filter	Θέλω τσιγάρα μέ/χωρίς φίλτρο thelo tsighara me/horis filtro
A box of large/small cigars	Ἔνα κουτί μέ μεγάλα/μικρά ποῦρα ena kouti me meghala/mikra poura
A box of matches	Ἔνα κουτί σπίρτα ena kouti spirta
I want to buy a lighter	Θέλω ν'ἀγοράσω ἔναν ἀναπτήρα thelo n'aghorasso enan anaptira
Do you sell lighter fuel ?	Ἔχετε βενζίνη γι'ἀναπτῆρες; ehete venzini ghia anaptires
I want a gas refill for this lighter	Θέλω ἔνα ἀνταλλακτικό μέ ἀέριο γ'αὐτόν τόν ἀναπτήρα thelo ena antalaktiko me aerio ghiafton ton anaptira

Newspapers, books, writing materials

Do you sell English/American newspapers?	Ἔχετε Ἀγγλικές/ Ἀμερικανικές ἐφημερίδες; ehete anglikes/amerikanikes efimeridhes
Can you get this magazine for me?	Μπορεῖτε νά μοῦ παραγγείλετε αὐτό τό περιοδικό; borite na mou parangilete afto to periodhiko
Where can I get the ...?	Ποῦ μπορῶ νά βρῶ τό ...; pou boro na vro to
I want a map of the city	Θέλω ἕνα χάρτη τῆς πόλης thelo ena harti tis polis
Do you have any English books?	Ἔχετε Ἀγγλικά βιβλία; ehete anglika vivlia
Have you any novels by ...?	Ἔχετε τίποτα μυθιστορήματα τοῦ ...; ehete tipota mithistorimata tou
I want some colour postcards	Θέλω μερικές ἔγχρωμες καρτποστάλ thelo merikes enhromes kartpostal

I want some black and white postcards/plain postcards

Θέλω ἀσπρόμαυρες/ἀπλές κάρτες
thelo aspromavres/aples kartes

Laundry, cleaning and mending

I want to have these things washed/ cleaned

Θέλω νά μοῦ πλύνετε/ καθαρίσετε αὐτά
thelo na mou plinete/ katharissete afta

These stains won't come out

*Αὐτοί οἱ λεκέδες δέ βγαίνουν
afti i lekedhes dhe vghenoun

It only needs to be pressed

Χρειάζεται μόνο σιδέρωμα
hriazete mono sidheroma

This is torn; can you mend it?

Αὐτό ἔχει σκιστεῖ. Μπορεῖτε νά τό μπαλώσετε;
afto ehi skisti. borite na to balossete

Do you do invisible mending?

Μαντάρετε χωρίς νά φαίνεται
mandarete horis na fenete

There's a button missing

Λείπει ἕνα κουμπί
lipi ena koumbi

Can you sew on a button here?	Μοῦ ράβετε αὐτό τό κουμπί; mou ravete afto to koumbi

Can you put in a new zip?	Μοῦ βάζετε ἕνα καινούργιο
	    φερμουάρ;
	mou vazete ena kenourghio
	    fermouar

When will they be ready?	Πότε θά 'ναι ἕτοιμα; pote tha ine etima
I need them by this evening/ tomorrow	Τά χρειάζομαι ἀπόψε/αὔριο ta hriazome apopse/avrio
Call back at 5 o'clock	*Γυρίστε στίς πέντε τ'ἀπόγευμα ghiriste stis pente t'apoghevma

We can do it by Thursday	*Μποροῦμε νά τό ἔχουμε ἕτοιμο
	    τή Πέμπτη
	boroume na to ehoume etimo
	    ti Pempti

It will take three days	*Θά πάρει τρεῖς μέρες tha pari tris meres

Repairs

SHOES

Can you sole these shoes with
leather ?

Μπορεῖτε νά μοῦ βάλετε
δερμάτινες σόλες;
borite na mou valete
dhermatines soles

Can you heel these shoes with
rubber ?

Μπορεῖτε νά μοῦ βάλετε
λαστιχένια τακούνια;
borite na mou valete lastihenia
takounia

I have broken the heel; can you put
on a new one ?

Ἔσπασε τό τακούνι. Μοῦ
βάζετε ἕνα καινούργιο;
espasse to takouni. mou vazete
ena kenourghio

Can you do them while I wait ?

Μπορεῖτε νά τά κάνετε ὅσο
περιμένω;
borite na ta kanete osso
perimeno

When should I pick them up ?

Πότε νά περάσω νά τά πάρω;
pote na perasso na ta
paro

WATCH/JEWELLERY

My watch is broken

Ἔσπασε τό ρολόϊ μου
espasse to roloi mou

My watch is always fast/slow	Τό ρολόϊ μου πηγαίνει ἐμπρός/πίσω to roloi mou pigheni embros/pisso
Can you repair it?	Μπορεῖτε νά τό σιάξετε; borite na to siaxete
I've broken the strap	Ἔσπασε τό λουράκι espasse to louraki
The fastener is broken	Ἔσπασε ἡ ἀγκράφα espasse i agrafa
How much will it cost?	Πόσο θά στοιχίση; posso tha stihissi
It can't be repaired	*Δέ διορθώνεται dhe dhiorthonete
You need a new one	*Χρειάζεστε ἕνα καινούργιο hriazeste ena kenourghio

BARBER AND HAIRDRESSER

May I make an appointment for tomorrow/this afternoon?	Μπορῶ νά κλείσω ἕνα ραντεβοῦ γιά αὔριο/σήμερα τ᾽ἀπόγευμα;
	boro na klisso ena rendezvous ghia avrio/simera tapoghevma
What time?	Τί ὥρα;
	ti ora
I want my hair cut/trimmed	Θέλω νά μοῦ κόψετε/νά μοῦ διορθώσετε λίγο τά μαλλιά
	thelo na mou kopsete/na mou dhiorthossete ligho ta malia
Not too short at the sides	"Οχι πολύ κοντά στό πλάϊ
	ohi poli konta sto plai
I'll have it shorter at the back	Λίγο πιό κοντά ἀπό πίσω
	ligho pio konta apo pisso
This is where I have my parting	Ἐδῶ εἶναι ἡ χωρίστρα μου
	edho ine i horistra mou
My hair is oily/dry	Τά μαλλιά μου εἶναι λιπαρά/ξερά
	ta malia mou ine lipara/xera
I want a shampoo	Θέλω σαμπού
	thelo shampoo
I want my hair washed and set	Θέλω νά μοῦ πλύνετε τά μαλλιά καί νά μοῦ κάνετε μιζαμπλί
	thelo na mou plinete ta malia ke na mou kanete mizampli

Please set it without rollers/with large/small rollers	Μιζαμπλί χωρίς ρολά παρακαλῶ/μέ μεγάλα/ μικρά ρολά **mizampli horis rola parakalo/ me meghala/mikra rola**
I'd like it set this way	Θέλω νά μοῦ τά τυλίξετε ἔτσι **thelo na mou ta tilixete etsi**
Have you any lacquer?	Ἔχετε λάκα; **ehete laka**
The water is too cold	Τό νερό εἶναι πολύ κρύο **to nero ine poli krio**
The dryer is too hot	Τό σεσουάρ εἶναι πολύ ζεστό **to sessouar ine poli zesto**
Thank you, I like it very much	Εὐχαριστῶ, μ'ἀρέσει πάρα πολύ **efharisto, maressi parapoli**
I want a shave/manicure	Θέλω νά μέ ξυρίσετε/manicure **thelo na me xirissete/manicure**
Shave and hair cut	Ξύρισμα καί κούρεμα **xirisma ke kourema**

POST OFFICE

Where's the main post office?	Ποῦ εἶναι τό κεντρικό ταχυδρομεῖο; pou ine to kentriko tahidhromio
Where's the nearest post office?	Ποῦ εἶναι τό πλησιέστερο ταχυδρομεῖο; pou ine to plissiestero tahidhromio
What time does the post office close?	Τί ὥρα κλείνει τό ταχυδρομεῖο; ti ora klini to tahidhromio
Where's the post box?	Ποῦ εἶναι τό γραμματοκιβώτιο pou ine to ghramatokivotio

Letters and telegrams

How much is a letter to England?	Πόσο κάνει ἕνα γράμμα γιά τήν Ἀγγλία; posso kani ena ghrama ghia tin Anglia
What's the airmail/surface mail to the U.S.A.?	Πόσο κάνει ἕνα ἀεροπορικό/ ἁπλό γράμμα γιά τήν Ἀμερική; posso kani ena aeroporiko/ aplo ghramma ghia tin Ameriki

It's inland	Εἶναι ἐσωτερικοῦ ine essoterik**ou**
Give me three five drahma stamps, please	Δῶστε μου τρία γραμματόσημα τῶν πέντε δραχμῶν **dh**ostemou tria ghramatossima ton pente dhrahm**on**
I want to send this letter express	Θέλω νά στείλω αὐτό τό γράμμα κατεπεῖγον thelo na stilo af**to** to **gh**rama katepighon
I want to register this letter	Θέλω νά στείλω αὐτό τό γράμμα συστημμένο thelo na stilo af**to** to **gh**rama sistimeno
Two airmail forms	Δύο ἀεροπορικά ἔντυπα **dh**io aeroporik**a** entipa
Where is the poste restante section?	Ποῦ εἶναι τό poste restante; pou ine to poste restante
Are there any letters for me	Ἔχετε γράμματα γιά μένα; ehete ghramata ghia **me**na
What is your name?	*Πῶς λέγεστε; pos leg**he**ste
Have you any means of identification?	*Ἔχετε ταυτότητα; ehete taftotita

I want to send a telegram/reply paid/overnight	Θέλω νά στείλω ἕνα τηλε-γράφημα/μέ πληρωμένη ἀπάντηση/βραδυνό thelo na stilo ena tileghrafima/ me pliromeni apantissi/ vradhino
How much does it cost per word?	Πόσο κάνει ἡ λέξη; posso kani i lexi
Write the message here and your own name and address	*Γράψτε τό μύνημα ἐδῶ καί τό ὄνομα καί τή διεύθυνση σας ghrapste to minima edho ke tonoma ke ti dhiefthinssi sas

Telephoning

Where's the nearest phone box	Ποῦ εἶναι ὁ πλησιέστερος τηλεφωνικός θάλαμος; pou ine o plissiesteros tilefonikos thalamos
I want to make a phone call	Θέλω νά κάνω ἕνα τηλεφώνημα thelo na kano ena tilefonima
Please give me a token	Δῶστε μου μία τηλεφωνική μάρκα dhoste mou mia tilefoniki marka

Please get me ...	Σᾶς παρακαλῶ πᾶρτε μου ... sas parakalo parte mou
I want to telephone to England	Θέλω νά τηλεφωνήσω στήν Ἀγγλία thelo ne tilefonisso stin anglia
I want to make a personal call	Θέλω νά κάνω ἕνα προσωπικό τηλεφώνημα thelo na kano ena prossopiko tilefonima
I want to reverse the charges/call collect	Θέλω νά χρεωθῆ τό τηλεφώνημα στόν παραλήπτη thelo na hreothi to tilefonima ston paralipti
Hello	Ἐμπρός embros
I want extension 43	Θέλω ἐσωτερικό σαραντατρία thelo essoteriko sarantatria
May I speak to ...	Μπορῶ νά μιλήσω στόν boro na milisso ston
Who's speaking?	*Ποιός μιλεῖ; pios mili
Hold the line, please	*Περιμένετε παρακαλῶ perimenete parakalo
Put the receiver down	*Κατεβάστε τό ἀκουστικό katevaste to akoustiko

He's not here	*Δέν εἶναι ἐδῶ dhen ine edho
He's at ...	*Εἶναι στό ... ine sto
When will he be back?	Πότε θά ἐπιστρέψη; pote tha epistrepsi
Will you take a message?	Μπορεῖτε νά πάρετε μία παραγγελία; borite na parete mia parangelia
Tell him that ... phoned	Πέστε του ὅτι τηλεφώνησε ὁ... peste tou oti tilefonisse o
Please ask him to phone me	Πέστε του σᾶς παρακαλῶ νά μοῦ τηλεφωνήση peste tou sas parakalo na mou tilefonissi
What's your number?	*Ποιός εἶναι ὁ ἀριθμός σας; pios ine o arithmos sas
My number is ...	Ὁ ἀριθμός μου εἶναι ... o arithmos mou ine
I can't hear you	Δέν σᾶς ἀκούω dhen sas akouo
The line is engaged	*Ἡ γραμμή εἶναι κατειλημμένη i ghrami ine katilimeni
There's no reply	*Δέν ἀπαντάει κανείς dhen apantai kanis
You have the wrong number	*Δέν ἔχετε τό σωστό ἀριθμό dhen ehete ton sosto arithmo

Telephone directory	Τηλεφωνικός κατάλογος
	tilefonikos kataloghos
Telephone number	Ἀριθμός τηλεφώνου
	arithmos tilefonou
Telephone operator (male/female)	Τηλεφωνητής (τηλεφωνήτρια)
	tilefonitis (tilefonitria)

SIGHTSEEING[1]

What ought one to see here?	Τί θά ἔπρεπε νά δῆ κανείς ἐδῶ; ti tha eprepe na dhi kanis edho
What's this building?	Τί εἶναι αὐτό τό κτίριο; ti ine afto to ktirio
Which is the oldest building in the city?	Ποιό εἶναι τό παλιώτερο κτίριο στή πόλη; pio ine to paliotero ktirio sti poli
When was it built?	Πότε κτίστηκε; pote ktistike
Who built it?	Ποιός τό'κτισε; pios toktisse
What's the name of this church?	Πῶς λέγεται αὐτή ἡ ἐκκλησία; pos leghete afti i eklissia
What time is mass at the Catholic church?	Τί ὥρα εἶναι ἡ λειτουργία στήν καθολική ἐκκλησία; ti ora ine i litourghia stin katholiki eklissia
What time is the service at the Orthodox Church/Synagogue?	Τί ὥρα εἶναι ἡ λειτουργία στήν ὀρθόδοξο ἐκκλησία/ θυναγωγή; ti ora ine i litourghia stin orthodhoxo eklissia/ sinaghoghi

1. See also TRAVEL (Bus or Coach), (p. 50) and DIRECTIONS (p. 55).

When is the museum open?	Πότε εἶναι ἀνοικτό τό μουσεῖο;
	pote ine anikto to moussio
Is it open on Sundays?	Εἶναι ἀνοικτό τίς Κυριακές;
	ine anikto tis kiriakes
The museum is closed on Mondays	*Τό μουσεῖο εἶναι κλειστό τίς Δευτέρες
	to moussio ine klisto tis dhefteres
Admission free	*Εἴσοδος ἐλευθέρα
	issodhos elefthera
How much is it to go in?	Πόσο κάνει ἡ εἴσοδος;
	posso kani i issodhos
Have you a ticket?	*Ἔχετε εἰσιτήριο;
	ehete issitirio
Where do I buy tickets?	Ποῦ ἀγοράζει κανείς εἰσιτήρια;
	pou aghorazi kanis issitiria
Please leave your bag in the cloak-room	*Ἀφῆστε τήν τσάντα σας στή γκαρνταρόμπα
	afiste tintsanta sas sti gardaroba
It's over there	*Εἶναι ἐκεῖ
	ine eki
Can I take pictures?	Μπορῶ νά φωτογραφίσω;
	boro na fotoghrafisso
Photographs are prohibited	*Ἀπαγορεύονται οἱ φωτογραφίες
	apaghorevonte i fotoghrafies

Follow the guide   *'Ακολουθήστε τόν όδηγό
      akolouthiste ton odhigho

Does the guide speak English ?   Μιλάει 'Αγγλικά ό όδηγός;
      milai anglika o odhighos

I don't need a guide   Δέ χρειάζομαι όδηγό
      dhen hriazome odhigho

Where is the . . . collection/   Ποῦ εἶναι ἡ συλλογή . . ./
     exhibition ?   ἡ ἔκθεση . . .
      pou ine i siloghi . . ./i
      ekthessi

Where can I get a catalogue ?   Ποῦ μπορῶ ν'άγοράσω ἕνα
      κατάλογο;
      pou boro naghorasso ena
      katalogho

Where can I get a map/guide book   Ποῦ μπορῶ ν'άγοράσω ἕνα
     of the city ?   χάρτη/όδηγό τῆς πόλης;
      pou boro naghorasso ena
      harti/odhigho tis polis

Is this the way to the zoo ?   Αὐτός εἶναι ὁ δρόμος γιά τόν
      ζωολογικό κῆπο;
      aftos ine o dhromos ghia ton
      zoologhiko kipo

Which bus goes to the castle ?   Ποιό λεωφορεῖο πηγαίνει στό
      κάστρο;
      pio leoforio pigheni sto kastro

Which is the way to the park ?   Πῶς πάει κανείς στό πάρκο;
      pos pai kanis sto parko

Can we walk there?

Μπορούμε νά τό περπατή-
σουμε;
boroume na to perpatissoume

ENTERTAINMENT

What's on at the theatre/cinema?	Τί παίζει στό θέατρο/ στόν κινηματόγραφο; ti pezi sto theatro/ston kinimatoghrafo
Is there a concert on this evening?	Έχει καμμιά συναυλία ἀπόψε; ehi kamia sinavlia apopse
I want two seats for tonight/the matinee tomorrow	Θέλω δύο θέσεις γι'ἀπόψε/ γιά τήν ἀπογευματινή παράσταση αὔριο thelo dhio thessis ghia apopse/ ghia tin apoghematini parastassi avrio
I want to book seats for Thursday	Θέλω νά κλείσω θέσεις γιά τήν Πέμπτη thelo na klisso thessis ghia tin pempti
Where are these seats?	Ποῦ εἶναι αὐτές οἱ θέσεις; pou ine aftes i thessis
What time does the performance start?	Τί ὥρα ἀρχίζει ἡ παράσταση; ti ora arhizi i parastassi
What time does it end?	Τί ὥρα τελειώνει; ti ora telioni
A programme, please	Ἕνα πρόγραμμα παρακαλῶ ena proghrama parakalo

Where are the best nightclubs?   Ποῦ εἶναι τά καλύτερα
                                                νυκτερινά κέντρα;
                                                pou ine ta kalitera nikterina
                                                kentra

What time is the floorshow?   Τί ὥρα ἀρχίζει τό πρόγραμμα;
                                                ti ora arhizi to proghrama

May I have this dance?   Θέλετε νά χορέψουμε;
                                                thelete na horepsoume

Is there a discotheque here?   Ὑπάρχει ἐδῶ καμμία
                                                χωρευτικό κέντρο /
                                                discotheque;
                                                iparhi edho kamia horeftiko
                                                kentro/discotheque

SPORTS AND GAMES

Where is the football stadium?	Ποῦ εἶναι τό γήπεδο τοῦ ποδοσφαίρου;
	pou ine to ghipedho tou podhosferou
Are there any seats in the grandstand?	Ὑπάρχουν θέσεις στίς κερκίδες;
	iparhoun thessis stis kerkidhes
How much are they?	Πόσο κάνουν;
	posso kanoun
Which are the cheapest seats?	Ποιές εἶναι οἱ πιό φθηνές θέσεις;
	pies ine i pio fthines thessis
Are the seats in the sun/shade?	Εἶναι αὐτές οἱ θέσεις στόν ἥλιο/ στή σκιά;
	ine aftes i thessis ston ilio/ sti skia
We want to go to a football match	Θέλουμε νά πᾶμε σ᾽ἕνα ποδοσφαιρικό match
	theloume na pame sena podhosferiko match
Who's playing?	Ποιός παίζει;
	pios pezi
When does it start?	Πότε ἀρχίζει;
	pote arhizi
Where's the race course?	Ποῦ εἶναι ὁ ἱππόδρομος;
	pou ine o ipodhromos

ON THE BEACH

Where are the best beaches?	Ποῦ εἶναι οἱ καλύτερες πλάζ; pou ine i kaliteres plaz
Is there a quiet beach near here?	Ὑπάρχει καμμιά ἥσυχη παραλία ἐδῶ κοντά; iparhi kamia issihi paralia edho konta
Can we walk or is it too far?	Μπορούμε νά πᾶμε μέ τά πόδια ἤ εἶναι πολύ μακρυά; boroume na pame me ta podhia i ine poli makria
Is there a bus to the beach?	Ἔχει λεωφορεῖο γιά τήνπλάζ; ehi leoforio ghia tin plaz
Is the beach sandy or rocky?	Εἶναι ἡ παραλία μέ βράχεια ἤ μέ ἄμμο; ine paralia me vrahia i me amo
Is it dangerous to bathe here?	Εἶναι ἐπικίνδυνο νά κολυμπήση κανείς ἐδῶ; ine epikindhino na kolimbissi kanis edho
Bathing prohibited	*Ἀπαγορεύεται ἡ κολύμβηση apaghorevete i kolimvissi
Diving prohibited	*Ἀπαγορεύονται οἱ βουτιές apaghorevonte i vouties
It's dangerous	*Εἶναι ἐπικίνδυνο ine epikindhino
There's a strong current here	*Ἔχει πολύ δυνατό ρεῦμα ἐδῶ ehi poli dhinato revma edho

Are you a strong swimmer?	*Εἶσαι καλός κολυμβητής; isse kalos kolimvitis
Is it deep?	Εἶναι βαθύ; ine vathi
How's the water?	Πῶς εἶναι τό νερό; pos ine to nero
It's warm/cold	Εἶναι ζεστό/κρύο ine zesto/krio
Can one swim in the lake?	Μπορεῖ κανείς νά κολυμπήση στή λίμνη; bori kanis na kolimbissi sti limni
Is there an indoor/outdoor swimming pool?	Ὑπάρχει κλειστή/ ἀνοικτή πισίνα; iparhi klisti/anikti pissina
Is it salt or fresh water?	Εἶναι μέ θαλασσινό ἤ μέ γλυκό νερό; ine me thalassino i me ghliko nero
Are there showers?	Ὑπάρχουν ντούς; iparhoun douche
I want a cabin for the day/for the morning/for two hours	Θέλω μιά καμπίνα γιά ὅλη τή μέρα/γιά τό πρωΐ /γιά δύο ὧρες thelo mia cabina ghia oli ti mera/ghia to proi/ghia dhio ores

I want to hire a deckchair/sunshade	Θέλω νά νοικιάσω μιά σεζλόγκ/ όμπρέλλα
	thelo na nikiasso mia chaise longue/umbrella
Can we water ski here?	Μπορούμε νά κάνουμε θαλάσσιο σκί έδῶ;
	boroume na kanoume thalassio ski edho
Can we hire the equipment?	Μπορούμε νά νοικιάσουμε τά ἀπαραίτητα;
	boroume na nikiassoume ta aparetita
Where's the harbour?	Ποῦ εἶναι τό λιμάνι;
	pou ine to limani
Can we go out in a fishing boat?	Μπορούμε νά πᾶμε μέ βάρκα;
	boroume na pame me varka
We want to go fishing	Θέλουμε νά πᾶμε γιά ψάρεμα
	theloume na pame ghia psarema
Is there any underwater fishing?	Ἔχει καθόλου ὑποβρύχειο ψάρεμμα;
	ehi katholou ipovrihio psarema
Can I hire a boat?	Μπορῶ νά νοικιάσω μιά βάρκα;
	boro na nikiasso mia varka
What does it cost by the hour?	Πόσο κάνει τήν ὥρα;
	posso kani tin ora

CAMPING AND WALKING[1]

How long is the walk to the Youth Hostel?	Πόσο ἀπέχει ὁ Ξενώνας τῶν Νέων; posso apehi o xenonas ton neon
How far is the next village?	Πόσο ἀπέχει τό ἐπόμενο χωριό; posso apehi to epomeno horio
Is there a footpath to . . .?	Ὑπάρχει μονοπάτι γιά τό . . .; iparhi monopati ghia to
Is there a short cut?	Μπορεῖ νά κόψη κανείς δρόμο; bori na kopsi kanis dhromo
It's an hour's walk to . . .	*Εἶναι μιά ὥρα μέ τά πόδια γιά τό . . . ine mia ora me ta podhia ghia to
Is there a camping site near here?	Ὑπάρχει κανένας χῶρος κατασκηνώσεως ἐδῶ κοντά; iparhi kanenas horos kataskinosseos edho konta
Is there drinking water?	Ὑπάρχει πόσιμο νερό; iparhi possimo nero
Are there sanitary arrangements/ showers?	*Ἔχει τουαλέτες/ντούς; ehi toualetes/douche
May we camp here?	Μπορούμε νά κατασκηνώσουμε ἐδῶ; boroume na kataskinossoume edho

1. See also DIRECTIONS (p. 55).

Can we hire a tent ?	Μπορούμε νά νοικιάσουμε μιά τέντα;
	boroume na nikiassoume mia tenda
Can we park our caravan here ?	Μπορούμε νά σταθμεύσουμε ἐδῶ;
	boroume na stathmefssoume edho
Is this drinking water ?	Εἶναι πόσιμο αὐτό τό νερό;
	ine possimo afto to nero
Where are the shops ?	Ποῦ εἶναι τά καταστήματα;
	pou ine ta katastimata
Where can I buy paraffin/butane gas ?	Ποῦ μπορῶ ν'ἀγοράσω πετρέλαιο/γκάζι;
	pou boro naghorasso petreleo/gazi
May we light a fire ?	Μπορούμε ν'ἀνάψουμε φωτιά;
	boroume nanapsoume fotia
Where do I dispose of rubbish ?	Ποῦ μπορῶ νά πετάξω τά σκουπίδια;
	pou boro na petaxo ta skoupidhia

AT THE DOCTOR'S

I must see a doctor; can you recommend one ?	Πρέπει νά δῶ ἕνα γιατρό. Μπορεῖτε νά μοῦ συστήσετε ἕναν; prepi na dho ena ghiatro. borite na mou sistissete enan
Please call a doctor	Φωνάξτε σᾶς παρακαλῶ ἕνα γιατρό fonaxte sas parakalo ena ghiatro
I am ill	Εἶμαι ἄρρωστος ime arostos
I've a pain in my right arm	Μοῦ πονάει τό δεξί μου χέρι mou ponai to dhexi mou heri
My wrist hurts	Μοῦ πονάει ὁ καρπός τοῦ χεριοῦ μου mou ponai o karpos tou heriou mou
I think I've sprained/broken my ankle	Νομίζω ὅτι ἔχω στραμπουλήξει/σπάσει τόν ἀστράγαλο μου nomizo oti eho stramboulixi/ spassi ton astraghalo mou
I fell down and hurt my back	Ἔπεσα καί κτύπησα τή πλάτη μου epessa ke ktipissa ti plati mou
My feet are swollen	Τά πόδια μου εἶναι πρισμένα ta podhia mou ine prismena

I've burned/cut/bruised myself	Κάηκα/κόπηκα/μωλωπίστηκα **kaika/kopika/molopistika**
My stomach is upset	Τό στομάχι μου εῖναι χαλασ- μένο **to stomahi mou ine halasmeno**
I have indigestion	Ἔχω δυσπεψία **eho dhispepsia**
My appetite's gone	Δέν ἔχω ὄρεξη **dhen eho orexi**
I think I've got food poisoning	Νομίζω πώς ἔπαθα τροφική δηλητηρίαση **nomizo pos epatha trofiki dhilitiriassi**
I can't eat/sleep	Δέ μπορῶ νά φάω/νά κοιμηθῶ **dhe boro na fao/na kimitho**
I am a diabetic	Ἔχω διαβήτη **eho dhiaviti**
My nose keeps bleeding	Ἡ μύτη μου ἀνοίγει συνεχῶς **i miti mou anighi sinehos**
I have earache	Μοῦ πονᾶν τ'αὐτιά μου **mou ponan taftia mou**
I have difficulty in breathing	Ἀναπνέω μέ δυσκολία **anapneo me dhiskolia**
I feel dizzy	Ζαλίζομαι **zalizome**

I feel sick	Αισθάνομαι ἄρρωστος esthanome arostos
I keep vomiting	Κάνω συνεχῶς ἐμετό kano sinehos emeto
I have a temperature	Ἔχω πυρετό eho pireto
I think I've caught 'flu	Νομίζω πῶς ἔπαθα γρίππη nomizo pos epatha ghripi
I've got a cold	Κρυολόγησα kriologhissa
I've had it since yesterday	Τό ἔχω ἀπό χθές to eho apo hthes
I've had it for a few hours	Τό ἔχω μερικές ὧρες τώρα to eho merikes ores tora
You're hurting me	Πονάω ponao
Must I stay in bed?	Πρέπει νά μείνω στό κρεβάτι; prepi na mino sto krevati
Will you come and see me again?	Θά 'ρθετε νά μέ ξαναδεῖτε; tharthete na me xanadhite
How much do I owe you?	Τί σᾶς ὠφείλω; ti sas ofilo
When do you think I can leave?	Πότε μπορῶ νά φύγω; pote boro na figho
I feel better now	Αισθάνομαι καλύτερα τώρα esthanome kalitera tora

Where does it hurt?	*Ποῦ πονάει; pou ponai
Have you a pain here?	*Πονᾶτε ἐδῶ; ponate edho
How long have you had the pain/ been suffering from . . . ?	*'Απὸ πότε ἀρχίσατε νὰ πονᾶτε/ νὰ ὑποφέρετε ἀπό . . . ; pote arhissate na ponate/na ipoferete apo . . .
Open your mouth	*'Ανοῖξτε τὸ στόμα σας anixte to stoma sas
Put out your tongue	*Βγᾶλτε τὴ γλῶσσα σας vghalte ti ghlossa sas
Breathe in	*Εἰσπνεῦστε ispnefste
Hold your breath	*Κρατῆστε τὴν ἀναπνοή σας kratiste tin anapnoi sas
Does that hurt?	*Πονάει; ponai
A lot or a little?	*Πολὺ ἢ λίγο poli i ligho
Lie down	*Ξαπλῶστε xaploste
Take these pills/medicine	*Πάρτε αὐτὰ τὰ χάπια/τὸ φάρμακο parte afta ta hapia/to farmako

Take this prescription to the chemist's	*Πάρτε αὐτή τή συνταγή στό φαρμακεῖο parte afti ti sintaghi sto farmakio
Take this three times a day	*Πάρτε το τρεῖς φορές τή μέρα parteto tris fores ti mera
I'll give you an injection	*Θά σᾶς κάνω μία ἔνεση tha sas kano mia enessi
Roll up your sleeve	*'Ανεβάστε τό μανίκι σας anevaste to maniki sas
You should stay on a diet for a few days	*Πρέπει νά κάνετε δίαιτα γιά λίγες μέρες prepi na kaneta dhieta ghia lighes meres
Come and see me again in two days' time	*'Ελᾶτε νά μέ ξαναδεῖτε σέ δύο μέρες elate na me xanadhite se dhio meres
Your leg must be X-rayed	*Πρέπει νά γίνη μιά ἀκτινογραφία τοῦ ποδιοῦ σας prepi na ghini mia aktinoghrafia tou podhiou sas
You must go to hospital	*Πρέπει νά πᾶτε στό νοσοκομεῖο prepi na pate sto nossokomio
You must stay in bed for a few days	*Πρέπει νά μείνετε στό κρεββάτι γιά λίγες μέρες prepi na minete sto krevati ghia lighes meres

abscess	ἀπόστημα **apostima**
allergy	ἀλλεργία **alerghia**
anaesthetic	ἀναισθητικό **anesthitiko**
appendicitis	σκωληκοειδῖτις **skolikoidhitis**
arthritis	ἀρθρῖτις **arthritis**
brain	μυαλό **mialo**
chiropodist	ποδίατρος **podhiatros**
constipation	δυσκοιλιότητα **dhiskiliotita**
diabetes	διαβήτης **dhiavitis**
diarrhoea	διάρροια **dhiaria**
earache	πόνος αὐτιῶν **ponos aftion**
false teeth	ὀδοντοστοιχία **odhondostihia**
fever	πυρετός **piretos**

filling (*tooth*)	βούλωμα **vouloma**
food poisoning	τροφική δηλητηρίασις **trofiki dhilitiriassis**
gum	ούλο **oulo**
hay fever	αλεργία **alerghia**
heart	καρδιά **kardhia**
heart condition	καρδιακή πάθησις **kardhiaki pathissis**
infection	μόλυνσις **molinssis**
influenza	γρίππη **ghripi**
injection	ένεση **enessi**
insomnia	αϋπνία **aipnia**
kidney	νεφρό **nefro**
liver	σηκώτι **sikoti**
lung	πνεύμονας **pnevmonas**

muscle	μῦς mis
nerve	νεῦρο nevro
pain	πόνος ponos
rheumatism	ρευματισμός revmatismos
sore throat	ἐρεθισμένος λαιμός/πονόλαιμος erethismenos lemos/ponolemos
stomach-ache	πόνος στομαχιοῦ ponos stomahiou
temperature	πυρετός piretos
thermometer	θερμόμετρο thermometro
tonsils	ἀμυγδαλές amighdhales
X-ray	ἀκτινογραφία aktinoghrafia

AT THE DENTIST'S

I must see a dentist	Πρέπει νά δῶ ἕναν ὁδοντογιατρό prepi na dho enan odhontoghiatro
Can I make an appointment with the dentist?	Μπορῶ νά κλείσω ἕνα ραντεβοῦ μέ τόν ὁδοντογιατρό; boro na klisso ena rendezvous me ton odhontoghiatro
As soon as possible	Ὅσο τό δυνατόν συντομώτερα osso to dhinaton sintomotera
I have toothache	Ἔχω πονόδοντο eho ponodhonto
This tooth hurts	Μοῦ πονάει αὐτό τό δόντι mou ponai afto to dhonti
I've lost a filling	Μοῦ ἔφυγε ἕνα βούλωμα mou efighe ena vouloma
Can you fill it?	Μπορεῖτε νά μοῦ τό βουλώσετε; borite na mou to voulossete
Can you do it now?	Μπορεῖτε νά τό κάνετε τώρα; borite na to kanete tora
Must you take the tooth out?	Εἶναι ἀπαραίτητο νά βγῆ τό δόντι; ine aparetito na vghi to dhonti

Please give me an injection first	Κάντε μου μία ἔνεση πρώτα σᾶς παρακαλῶ **kante mou mia enessi prota sas parakalo**
My gums are swollen/ keep bleeding	Τά οὔλα μου εἶναι πρισμένα/ ματώνουν ta **oula** mou **ine** prismena/ matonoun
I've broken my plate, can you repair it?	Ἔσπασα τήν ὀδοντοστοιχία μου. Μπορεῖτε νά μοῦ τή διορθώσετε; espassa tin odhontostihia mou. borite na mou ti dhiorthossete
You're hurting me	Μέ πονᾶτε me ponate
How much do I owe you?	Τί σᾶς ὀφείλω; ti sas ofilo
When should I come again?	Πότε νά ξανάρθω; pote na ksanartho
Please rinse your mouth	*Παρακαλῶ ξεπλύντε τό στόμα σας parakalo kseplinte to stoma sas
I will X-ray your teeth	*Θά σᾶς κάνω μία ἀκτινογραφία τῶν δοντιῶν σας tha sas kano mia aktinoghrafia ton dhontion sas

You have an abscess

*Ἔχετε ἕνα ἀπόστημα
ehete ena apostima

The nerve is exposed

*Τό νεῦρο εἶναι ἐκτεθειμένο
to nevro ine ektethimeno

This tooth will have to come out

*Αὐτό τό δόντι πρέπει νά βγῆ
afto to dhonti prepi na vghi

PROBLEMS AND ACCIDENTS

Where's the police station?
Ποῦ εἶναι ἡ ἀστυνομία;
pou ine i astinomia

Call the police
Φωνάξτε τήν ἀστυνομία
fonaxte tin astinomia

Where is the British/American consulate?
Ποῦ εἶναι τό ᾿Αγγλικό/
᾿Αμερικανικό Προξενεῖο;
pou ine to angliko/
amerikaniko proxenio

Please let the consulate know
Σᾶς παρακαλῶ εἰδοποιεῖστε
τόν Πρόξενο
sas parakalo idhopiiste ton proxeno

My bag/wallet has been stolen
῾Η τσάντα/τό πορτοφόλι μου
ἐκλάπησαν
i tsanta/to portofoli mou eklapissan

I found this in the street
Τό βρῆκα στό δρόμο
to vrika sto dhromo

I have lost my luggage/passport/ travellers' cheques
῎Εχασα τίς ἀποσκευές/
διαβατήριο/travellers'
cheques μου
ehassa tis aposkeves/
dhiavatirio/travellers'
cheques mou

I have missed my train
῎Εχασα τό τραῖνο μου
ehassa to treno mou

My luggage is on board	Οἱ ἀποσκευές μου ἔχουν ἐπιβιβασθεῖ i aposkeves mou ehoun epivivasthi
Call a doctor	Φωνάξτε ἕνα γιατρό fonaxte ena ghiatro
Call an ambulance	Φωνάξτε ἕνα φορεῖο fonaxte ena forio
There has been an accident	Συνέβη ἕνα ἀτύχημα sinevi ena atihima
He's badly hurt	Εἶναι σοβαρά τραυματισμένος ine sovara travmatismenos
He has fainted	Λιποθύμησε lipothimisse
He's losing blood	Αἱμορραγεῖ emoraghi
Please get some water/a blanket/ some bandages	Σᾶς παρακαλῶ φέρτε λίγο νερό/μία κουβέρτα/ ἐπιδέσμους sas parakalo ferte ligho nero/ mia kouverta/epidhesmous
I've broken my glasses	Ἔσπασα τά γυαλιά μου espassa ta ghialia mou
I can't see	Δέν βλέπω dhen vlepo

A child has fallen in the water	Ἕνα παιδάκι ἔπεσε μέσ᾽στό νερό
	ena pedhaki epesse messto nero
May I see your insurance policy?	*Μπορῶ νά δῶ τήν ἀσφάλεια σας;
	boro na dho tin asfalia sas
Apply to the insurance company	*Ρωτῆστε τήν ἀσφάλεια
	rotiste tin asfalia
I want a copy of the police report	Θέλω ἕνα ἀντίγραφο τῆς ἀστυνομικῆς ἀναφορᾶς
	thelo ena antighrafo tis astinomikis anaforas

TIME AND DATES

What time is it ?	Τί ὥρα εἶναι; ti ora ine
It's one o'clock	Εἶναι μία ἡ ὥρα ine mia i ora
2 o'clock	δύο ἡ ὥρα dhio i ora
midday	Μεσημέρι messimeri
midnight	Μεσάνυκτα messanikta
quarter to ten	Δέκα παρά τέταρτο dheka para tetarto
quarter past five	Πέντε καί τέταρτο pente ke tetarto
half past four	τέσσερις καί μισή tesseris ke missi
five past eight	ὀκτώ καί πέντε okto ke pente
twenty to three	τρεῖς παρά εἴκοσι tris para ikossi
It's early/late	Εἶναι νωρίς/ἀργά ine noris/argha
My watch is slow/fast/has stopped	Τό ρολόϊ μου πάει σιγά/ γρήγορα/σταμάτησε to roloi mou pai sigha/ ghrighora/stamatisse

What time does it start/finish?	Τί ὥρα ἀρχίζει/τελειώνει; ti ora arhizi/telioni
Are you staying long?	Θά μείνετε πολύ; tha minete poli
I'm staying for two weeks/four days	Θά μείνω δύο ἑβδομάδες/ τέσσερις μέρες tha mino dhio evdhomadhes/ tesseris meres
I've been here for a week	Εἶμαι ἤδη ἐδῶ δύο ἑβδομάδες ime idhi edho dhio evdhomadhes
We're leaving on 5th January	Φεύγουμε στίς πέντε 'Ιανουαρίου fevghoume stis pente ianouariou
We got here on 27th July	Φτάσαμε ἐδῶ στίς εἴκοσι-ἑπτά 'Ιουλίου ftassame edho stis ikossiepta iouliou
What's the date?	Πόσες ἔχει ὁ μήνας; posses ehi o minas
It's 9th December	Εἶναι ἐννιά Δεκεμβρίου ine enia dhekemvriou
Today	Σήμερα simera
Yesterday	Χθές hthes

Tomorrow	Αὔριο avrio
Day after tomorrow	Μεθαύριο methavrio
Day before yesterday	Προχθές prohthes
Day	'Ημέρα imera
Morning	Πρωΐ proi
Afternoon	'Απόγευμα apoghevma
Evening	Νύκτα nikta
Night	Νύκτα nikta
This morning	Σήμερα τό πρωΐ simera to proi
Yesterday afternoon	Χθές τό ἀπόγευμα hthes to apoghevma
Tomorrow evening	Αὔριο τό βράδυ avrio to vradhi
In the morning	Τό πρωΐ to proi
In ten days' time	Σέ δέκα μέρες se dheka meres

On Tuesday	Τήν Τρίτη
	tin triti
On Sundays	Τίς Κυριακές
	tis kiriakes
This week	Αὐτή τήν ἑβδομάδα
	afti tin evdhomadha
Last month	Τόν περασμένο μῆνα
	ton perasmeno mina
Next year	Τοῦ χρόνου
	tou hronou
Sunday	Κυριακή
	kiriaki
Monday	Δευτέρα
	dheftera
Tuesday	Τρίτη
	triti
Wednesday	Τετάρτη
	tetarti
Thursday	Πέμπτη
	pempti
Friday	Παρασκευή
	paraskevi
Saturday	Σάββατο
	savato
January	'Ιανουάριος
	ianouarios

February	Φεβρουάριος
	fevrouarios
March	Μάρτιος
	martios
April	Ἀπρίλιος
	aprilios
May	Μάϊος
	maios
June	Ἰούνιος
	iounios
July	Ἰούλιος
	ioulios
August	Αὔγουστος
	avghoustos
September	Σεπτέμβριος
	septemvrios
October	Ὀκτώβριος
	oktovrios
November	Νοέμβριος
	noemvrios
December	Δεκέμβριος
	dhekemvrios

PUBLIC HOLIDAYS

25 Μαρτίου
ikosti pempti martiou

25th March: Independence Day

15 Αὐγούστου – Τῆς Παναγίας
dhekapente avghoustou – tis
   panaghias

15th August: The Annunciation

28 Ὀκτωβρίου
ikosti oghdhoi oktovriou

28th October: The *Ochi* day
   (Greece's refusal to surrender
   to Germany in 1940)

25 Δεκεμβρίου – Χριστούγεννα
ikosti pempti dhekemvriou –
   hristoughena

25th December: Christmas

31 Δεκεμβρίου – Παραμονή
   Πρωτοχρονιᾶς
triakosti proti dhekemvriou –
   paramoni protohronias

31st December: New Year's Eve

1 Ἰανουαρίου – Πρωτοχρονιά
proti ianouariou – protohronia

1st January: New Year's Day

Τό Ἅγιον Πάσχα
to aghion pasha

Easter

NUMBERS

CARDINAL

0	Μηδέν midhen	12	Δώδεκα dhodheka
1	Ἕνα ena	13	Δεκατρία dhekatria
2	Δύο dhio	14	Δεκατέσσερα dhekatessera
3	Τρία tria	15	Δεκαπέντε dhekapente
4	Τέσσερα tessera	16	Δεκαέξη dhekaexi
5	Πέντε pente	17	Δεκαεπτά dhekaepta
6	Ἕξη exi	18	Δεκαοκτώ dhekaokto
7	Ἑπτά epta	19	Δεκαεννέα dhekaenea
8	Ὀκτώ okto	20	Εἴκοσι ikossi
9	Ἐννέα enea	21	Εἰκοσιένα ikossiena
10	Δέκα dheka	22	Εἰκοσιδύο ikossidhio
11	Ἕνδεκα endheka	30	Τριάντα trianda

31	Τριανταένα triandaena	100	Ἑκατό ekato
40	Σαράντα saranda	101	Ἑκατονένα ekatonena
50	Πενῆντα peninda	200	Διακόσια dhiakossia
60	Ἑξῆντα exinda	1,000	Χίλια hilia
70	Ἑβδομῆντα evdhominta	2,000	Δύο χιλιάδες dhio hiliadhes
80	Ὀγδόντα oghdhonta	1,000,000	Ἕνα ἑκατομμύριο ena ekatomirio
90	Ἐνενῆντα eneninta		

ORDINAL

1st	Πρῶτος protos	6th	Ἕκτος ektos
2nd	Δεύτερος dhefteros	7th	Ἕβδομος evdhomos
3rd	Τρίτος tritos	8th	Ὄγδοος oghdhoos
4th	Τέταρτος tetartos	9th	Ἔνατος enatos
5th	Πέμπτος pemptos	10th	Δέκατος dhekatos

11th	'Ενδέκατος endhekatos	40th	Τεσσαρακοστός tessarakostos
12th	Δωδέκατος dhodhekatos	50th	Πεντηκοστός pentikostos
13th	Δέκατος τρίτος dhekatos tritos	60th	'Εξηκοστός exikostos
14th	Δέκατος τέταρτος dhekatos tetartos	70th	'Εβδομηκοστός evdhomikostos
15th	Δέκατος πέμπτος dhekatos pemptos	80th	'Ογδοηκοστός oghdhoikostos
16th	Δέκατος ἕκτος dhekatos ektos	90th	'Ενενηκοστός enenikostos
17th	Δέκατος ἕβδομος dhekatos evdhomos	100th	'Εκατοστός ekatostos
18th	Δέκατος ὄγδοος dhekatos oghdhoos	half	μισός missos
19th	Δέκατος ἕνατος dhekatos enatos	quarter	ἕν τέταρτον en tetarton
20th	Εἰκοστός ikostos	three quarters	τρία τέταρτα tria tetarta
21st	Εἰκοστός πρῶτος ikostos protos	a third	ἕν τρίτον en triton
30th	Τριακοστός triakostos	two thirds	δύο τρίτα dhio trita

WEIGHTS AND MEASURES

Distance: kilometres – miles

km.	miles or km.	miles		km.	miles or km.	miles
1·6	1	0·6		14·5	9	5·6
3·2	2	1·2		16·1	10	6·2
4·8	3	1·9		32·2	20	12·4
6·4	4	2·5		40·2	25	15·3
8	5	3·1		80·5	50	31·1
9·7	6	3·7		160·9	100	62·1
11·3	7	4·4		804·7	500	310·7
12·9	8	5·0				

A rough way to convert from miles to km.: divide by 5 and multiply by 8; from kg. to miles, divide by 8 and multiply by 5.

Length and height: centimetres – inches

cm.	ins or cm.	ins		cm.	ins or cm.	ins
2·5	1	0·4		17·8	7	2·8
5·1	2	0·8		20	8	3·2
7·6	3	1·2		22·9	9	3·5
10·2	4	1·6		25·4	10	3·9
12·7	5	2·0		50·8	20	7·9
15·2	6	2·4		127	50	19·7

A rough way to convert from inches to cm.: divide by 2 and multiply by 5; from cm. to inches, divide by 5 and multiply by 2.

metres – feet

m.	ft or m.	ft	m.	ft or m.	ft
0·3	1	3·3	2·4	8	26·3
0·6	2	6·6	2·7	9	29·5
0·9	3	9·8	3	10	32·8
1·2	4	13·1	6·1	20	65·6
1·5	5	16·4	15·2	50	164
1·8	6	19·7	30·5	100	328·1
2·1	7	23			

A rough way to convert from ft to m.: divide by 10 and multiply by 3; from m. to ft, divide by 3 and multiply by 10.

metres – yards

m.	yds or m.	yds	m.	yds or m.	yds
0·9	1	1·1	7·3	8	8·8
1·8	2	2·2	8·2	9	9·8
2·7	3	3·3	9·1	10	10·9
3·7	4	4·4	18·3	20	21·9
4·6	5	5·5	45·7	50	54·7
5·5	6	6·6	91·4	100	109·4
6·4	7	7·7	457·2	500	546·8

A rough way to convert from yds to m.: suntract 10 per cent from the number of yds; from m. to yds, add 10 per cent to the number of metres.

Liquid measures: litres – gallons

litres	galls or litres	galls		litres	galls or litres	galls
4·6	1	0·2		36·4	8	1·8
9·1	2	0·4		40·9	9	2·0
13·6	3	0·7		45·5	10	2·2
18·2	4	0·9		90·9	20	4·4
22·7	5	1·1		136·4	30	6·6
27·3	6	1·3		181·8	40	8·8
31·8	7	1·5		227·3	50	11

1 pint = 0·6 litre   1 litre = 1·8 pint

A rough way to convert from galls to litres: divide by 2 and multiply by 9; from litres to galls, divide by 9 and multiply by 2.

Weight: kilogrammes – pounds

kg.	lb. or kg.	lb.		kg.	lb. or kg.	lb.
0·5	1	2·2		3·2	7	15·4
0·9	2	4·4		3·6	8	17·6
1·4	3	6·6		4·1	9	19·8
1·8	4	8·8		4·5	10	22·1
2·3	5	11·0		9·1	20	44·1
2·7	6	13·2		22·7	50	110·2

A rough way to convert from lb. to kg.: divide by 11 and multiply by 5; from kg. to lb., divide by 5 and multiply by 11.

grammes – ounces

grammes	*oz.*	*oz.*	*grammes*
100	3·5	2	57·1
250	8·8	4	114·3
500	17·6	8	228·6
1,000 (1 kg.)	35	16 (1 lb.)	457·2

Temperature: centigrade – fahrenheit

centigrade °C	*fahrenheit* °F
0	32
5	41
10	50
20	59
30	86
40	104

A rough way to convert from °F to °C: deduct 32 and multiply by $\frac{5}{9}$; from °C to °F, multiply by $\frac{9}{5}$ and add 32.

VOCABULARY

Adjectives are given here in their masculine genders. Verbs are given in the first person singular of the present tense.

A

a, an *masc., fem., neut.*	ἕνας, μία, ἕνα	enas, mia, ena
able (to be)	μπορῶ	boro
about	περίπου	peripou
above	ἀπό πάνω	apo pano
abroad	ἐξωτερικό	exoteriko
accept (to)	δέχομαι	dhehome
accident	ἀτύχημα	atihima
ache	πόνος	ponos
acquaintance	γνωριμία	ghnorimia
across	διά μέσου	dhia messou
actor	ἠθοποιός	ithopios
actress	ἠθοποιός	ithopios
add	προσθέτω	prostheto
address	διεύθυνση	dhiefthinssi
advice	συμβουλή	simvouli
aeroplane	ἀεροπλάνο	aeroplano
afraid (to be)	φοβᾶμαι	fovame
after	μετά	meta
afternoon	ἀπόγευμα	apoghevma

again	ξανά	ksana
against	ἐναντίον	enantion
age	ἡλικία	ilikia
agency	πρακτορεῖο	praktorio
agent	πράκτωρ	praktor
ago	πρό, πρίν	pro, prin
agree (to)	συμφωνῶ	simfono
air	ἀέρας	aeras
air-conditioning	κλιματισμός	klimatismos
airline	ἀεροπορική γραμμή	aeroporiki ghrami
airmail	ἀεροπορικός	aeroporikos
airport	ἀεροδρόμιο	aerodhromio
all	ὅλοι	oli
allow (to)	ἐπιτρέπω	epitrepo
all right	ἐντάξει	entaxi
almost	σχεδόν	skhedhon
alone	μόνος	monos
along	κατά μῆκος	kata mikos
already	ἤδη	idhi
alter (to)	ἀλλάζω	alazo
although	ἄν καί	an ke
always	πάντα	panta

ambulance	νοσοκομειακό αὐτοκίνητο	nossokomiako aftokinito
American *adj.*	᾿Αμερικάνικος	amerikanikos
American *noun*	᾿Αμερικάνος	amerikanos
amuse (to)	διασκεδάζω	dhiaskedhazo
amusing	διασκεδαστικό	dhiaskedhastiko
ancient	ἀρχαῖος	arheos
and	καί	ke
angry	θυμωμένος	thimomenos
animal	ζῶον	zoon
ankle	ἀστράγαλος	astraghalos
another *masc.*, *fem.*, *neut.*	ἄλλος, ἄλλη, ἄλλο	alos, ali, alo
answer	ἀπάντηση	apantissi
answer (to)	ἀπαντῶ	apanto
antique	ἀρχαῖο	arheo
anyone *masc.*, *fem.*, *neut.*	ὁποιοσδήποτε, ὁποιαδήποτε, ὁποιοδήποτε	opiosdhipote opiadhipote, opiodhipote
anything	ὁτιδήποτε	otidhipote
anywhere	ὁπουδήποτε	opoudhipote
apartment	διαμέρισμα	dhiamerisma
apologize (to)	ζητῶ συγγνώμη	zito sighnomi
appetite	ὄρεξη	orexi

apple	μῆλο	milo
appointment	ραντεβοῦ	rendezvous
April	'Απρίλιος	aprilios
architect	ἀρχιτέκτονας	arhitektonas
architecture	ἀρχιτεκτονική	arhitektoniki
arm	μπράτσο	bratso
armchair	πολυθρόνα	polithrona
arrange (to)	τακτοποιῶ	taktopio
arrival	ἄφιξη	afixi
arrive (to)	φθάνω	fthano
art	τέχνη	tehni
art gallery	πινακοθήκη	pinakothiki
artist	καλλιτέχνης	kalitehnis
as	σάν	san
as much as	τόσο ὅσο	tosso osso
as soon as	μόλις	molis
as well	ἐπίσης	epissis
ashtray	σταχτοδοχεῖο	stahtodhohio
ask (to)	ρωτῶ	roto
asleep	κοιμισμένος	kimismenos
aspirin	ἀσπιρίνη	aspirini
at	στό	sto
at last	ἐπιτέλους	epitelous

at once	ἀμέσως	amessos
atmosphere	ἀτμόσφαιρα	atmosfera
attention	προσοχή	prossohi
August	Αὔγουστος	avghoustos
aunt	θεία	thia
Australia	Αὐστραλία	afstralia
Australian	Αὐστραλός	aftralos
author	συγγραφέας	singhrafeas
autumn	φθινόπωρο	fthinoporo
available	διαθέσιμος	dhiathessimos
awake	ξυπνῶ	ksipno
away *far*	μακρυά	makria

B

baby	μωρό	moro
back *adv.*	πίσω	pisso
back *noun*	πλάτη	plati
bad	κακός	kakos
bad *food*	χαλασμένο φαγητό	halasmeno faghito
bag	τσάντα	tsanta
baker	ψωμᾶς	psomas
balcony	μπαλκόνι	balkoni
ball *dance*	χορός	horos

ball *sport*	μπάλα	bala
ballpoint pen	μπίκ	bic
ballet	μπαλλέτο	baleto
banana	μπανάνα	banana
band *music*	μπάντα	banda
bandage	ἐπίδεσμος	epidhesmos
bank	τράπεζα	trapeza
bar	μπάρ	bar
barber	κουρέας	koureas
basket	καλάθι	kalathi
bath	μπάνιο	banio
bathe (to)	πλένομαι	plenome
bathing cap	σκούφια κολυμπήματος	skoufia kolimbimatos
bathing costume	μαγιώ	maghio
bathing trunks	μαγιώ	maghio
bathroom	μπάνιο	banio
battery	μπαταρία	bataria
bay	κόλπος	kolpos
be (to)	εἶμαι	ime
beach	ἀμμουδιά, παραλία	amoudhia, paralia
beard	γενειάδα	gheniadha
beautiful	ὡραῖος	oreos

because	γιατί	ghiati
bed	κρεββάτι	krevati
bedroom	κρεββατοκάμαρα	krevatokamara
beer	μπύρα	bira
before	πρίν	prin
begin (to)	άρχίζω	arhizo
beginning	άρχή	arhi
behind	άπό πίσω	apo pisso
believe (to)	πιστεύω	pistevo
bell	κουδούνι	koudhouni
belong (to)	άνήκω	aniko
below	άπό κάτω	apo kato
belt	ζώνη	zoni
berth	κουκέτα	kouketa
best	ό ποιό καλός	o pio kalos
better	καλύτερος	kaliteros
between	άνάμεσα	anamessa
bicycle	ποδήλατο	podhilato
big	μεγάλος	meghalos
bill	λυγαριασμός	loghariasmos
bird	πουλί	pouli
birthday	γενέθλια	ghenethlia
bite (to)	δαγκώνω	dhangono

black	μαῦρος	mavros
blanket	κουβέρτα	kouverta
bleach (to)	λευκαίνω, ξασπρίζω	lefkeno, ksasprizo
bleed (to)	ματώνω	matono
blister	φουσκάλα	fouskala
blood	αἷμα	ema
blouse	μπλούζα	blouza
blue	μπλέ	ble
(on) board	ἐπάνω στό πλοῖο	epano sto plio
boarding house	πανσιόν	pansion
boat *rowing boat*	βάρκα	varka
boat *steamer*	πλοῖο	plio
body	σῶμα	soma
bolster	μαξιλάρα	maxilara
bone	κόκκαλο	kokalo
book	βιβλίο	vivlio
book (to)	κλείνω	klino
booking office	ταμεῖο	tamio
bookshop	βιβλιοπωλεῖο	vivliopolio
borrow (to)	δανείζομαι	dhanizome
both	καί οἱ δύο	ke i dhio
bottle	μπουκάλι	boukali
bottle opener	τιρμπουσόν	tirbousson

bottom	πάτος	patos
bowl	κύπελλο	kipelo
box *container*	κουτί	kouti
box *theatre*	θεωρεῖο	theorio
box office	ταμεῖο	tamio
boy	ἀγόρι	aghori
bracelet	βραχιόλι	vrahioli
braces	τιράντες	tirantes
brandy	κονιάκ	coniac
brassiere	σουτιέν	soutien
bread	ψωμί	psomi
break (to)	σπάζω	spazo
breakfast	πρόγευμα	proghevma
breathe (to)	ἀναπνέω	anapneo
bridge	γέφυρα	ghefira
briefs	σώβρακα	sovraka
bright	λαμπερός	lamberos
bring (to)	φέρνω	ferno
British	Ἀγγλικό	angliko
broken	σπασμένος	spasmenos
brooch	ἀγκράφα	agrafa
brother	ἀδελφός	adhelfos
brown	καφέ	kafe

bruise	μελανιά	melania
bruise (to)	μωλωπίζω	molopizo
brush	βούρτσα	vourtsa
bucket	κουβάς	kouvas
build (to)	κτίζω	ktizo
building	κτίριο	ktirio
buoy	σημαδούρα	simadhoura
burn (to)	καίω	keo
burst (to)	ξεσπάω	xespao
bus	λεωφορείο	leoforio
bus stop	στάσις λεωφορείου	stassis leoforiou
business	ἐπιχείρησις	epihirissis
busy	ἀπασχολημένος	apaskholimenos
but	ἀλλά	ala
butane gas	πετρογκάζ	petrogaz
butcher	χασάπης	hassapis
butter	βούτυρο	voutiro
button	κουμπί	koumbi
buy (to)	ἀγοράζω	aghorazo
by	ἀπό	apo

C

| cabin | καμπίνα | cabina |

cable	καλώδιο	kalodhio
cafe	καφενεῖο	kafenio
cake	κέϊκ	cake
call (to) summon	καλῶ	kalo
call	φωνάζω	fonazo
call (to) (visit)	ἐπισκέπτομαι	episkeptome
camera	φωτογραφική μηχανή	fotoghrafiki mihani
camp (to)	κατασκηνώνω	kataskinono
camp site	χῶρος κατασκηνώσεως	horos kataskinoseos
can (to be able)	μπορῶ	boro
can (tin)	κονσέρβα	konsserva
Canada	Καναδάς	kanadhas
Canadian	Καναδός	kanadhos
cancel (to)	ἀκυρώνω	akirono
canoe	κανό	kano
cap	σκούφια	skoufia
capital city	πρωτεύουσα	protevoussa
car	αὐτοκίνητο	aftokinito
car licence	ἄδεια ὁδηγήσεως	adhia oghighisseos
car park	χῶρος σταθμεύσεως αὐτοκινήτων	horos stathmefsseos aftokiniton
carafe	καράφα	karafa

caravan	καραβάνι	karavani
careful	προσεκτικός	prosektikos
carry (to)	κουβαλῶ	kouvalo
cash (to)	ἐξαργυρώνω	exarghirono
cashier	ταμίας	tamias
casino	καζίνο	kazino
castle	κάστρο	kastro
cat	γάτα	ghata
catalogue	κατάλογος	kataloghos
catch (to)	πιάνω	piano
cathedral	μητρόπολις	mitropolis
catholic	καθολικός	katholikos
cave	σπηλιά	spilia
centre	κέντρο	kentro
century	αἰώνας	eonas
ceremony	τελετή	teleti
certain	βέβαιος	veveos
chair	καρέκλα	karekla
chambermaid	καμαριέρα	kamariera
champagne	σαμπάνια	sampania
(small) change	ψιλά	psila
change (to)	ἀλλάζω	alazo
charge	κόστος	kostos

charge (to)	χρεώνω	hreono
cheap	φθηνό	fthino
check (to)	ἐλέγχω	elenho
cheek	μάγουλο	maghoulo
cheese	τυρί	tiri
chemist	φαρμακοποιός	farmakopios
cheque	ἐπιταγή	epitaghi
chest	στῆθος	stithos
chicken	κοτόπουλο	kotopoulo
child	παιδί	pedhi
chill	κρύωμα	krioma
chin	πηγούνι	pighouni
china	γυαλικά	ghialika
chocolate	σοκολάτα	sokolata
Christmas	Χριστούγεννα	hristoughena
church	ἐκκλησία	eklissia
cigar	ποῦρο	pouro
cigarette	τσιγάρο	tsigharo
cigarette case	τσιγαροθήκη	tsigharothiki
cigarette lighter	ἀναπτήρας	anaptiras
cine camera	κινηματογραφική	kinimatoghrafiki
	μηχανή	mihani
cinema	κινηματόγραφος	kinimatoghrafos

circus	τσίρκο	tsirko
city	πόλη	poli
clean (to)	καθαρίζω	katharizo
clean	καθαρός	katharos
cliff	γκρεμνός	gremnos
cloakroom	γκαρνταρόμπα	gardaroba
clock	ρολόϊ	roloi
close (to)	κλείνω	klino
closed	κλειστό	klisto
cloth	ύφασμα	ifasma
clothes	ρούχα	rouha
coach	λεωφορείο	leoforio
coast	ἀκτή	akti
coat	παλτό	palto
coffee	καφές	kafes
coin	νόμισμα	nomisma
cold *adj.*	κρύο	krio
collar	κολλάρο	kolaro
collar stud	κουμπί κολλάρου	koumbi kolarou
colour	χρῶμα	hroma
colour film	ἔγγρωμο φίλμ	enhromo film
comb	κτένι	kteni
come (to)	ἔρχομαι	erhome

come in	ἐμπρός	embros
comfortable	ἀναπαυτικός	anapaftikos
compartment *train*	διαμέρισμα τραίνου	dhiamerisma trenou
complain (to)	διαμαρτύρομαι	dhiamartirome
complete	πλῆρες	plires
concert	συναυλία	sinavlia
conductor *bus*	εἰσπράκτωρ	ispraktor
conductor *orchestra*	μαέστρος	maestros
congratulations	συγχαρητήρια	sinharitiria
connection *train, etc.*	ἀνταπόκριση	antapokrissi
consul	πρόξενος	proxenos
consulate	προξενεῖο	proxenio
contain (to)	περιέχω	perieho
convenient	βολικός	volikos
convent	μοναστῆρι	monastiri
conversation	συζήτηση	sizitissi
cook	μάγειρας	maghiras
cook (to)	μαγειρεύω	maghirevo
cool	δροσερός	dhrosseros
copper	χαλκός	halkos
cork	φελλός	felos
corkscrew	τιρμπουσόν	tirbousson
corner	γωνία	ghonia

correct	σωστός	sostos
corridor	διάδρομος	dhiadhromos
cosmetics	καλλυντικά	kalintika
cost	κόστος, τιμή	kostos, timi
cost (to)	κοστίζω	kostizo
cotton	βαμβακερό	vamvakero
cotton wool	βαμβάκι	vamvaki
couchette	κουκέττα	kouketa
cough	βήχας	vihas
count (to)	μετρῶ	metro
country *nation*	χώρα	hora
country *not town*	ἐξοχή	exohi
cousin	ξάδελφος	ksadhelfos
cover charge	κουβέρ	couver
cramp	κράμπα	kramba
cream	κρέμα	krema
cross	σταυρός	stavros
cross (to)	σταυρώνω	stavrono
crossroads	σταυροδρόμι	stavrodhromi
cufflinks	μανικέτια	maniketia
cup	φλυτζάνι	flidzani
cupboard	ντουλάπι	doulapi
cure (to)	γιατρεύω	ghiatrevo

curl	μπούκλα	boukla
current	ρεῦμα	revma
curtain	κουρτίνα	kourtina
cushion	μαξιλάρι	maxilari
customs	τελωνεῖο	telonio
customs officer	τελωνειακός ὑπάλληλος	teloniakos ipalilos
cut	κόψιμο	kopsimo
cut (to)	κόβω	kovo

D

daily	καθημερινά	kathimerina
damaged	χαλασμένος	halasmenos
damp	ὑγρός	ighros
dance	χορός	horos
dance (to)	χορεύω	horevo
danger	κίνδυνος	kindhinos
dangerous	ἐπικίνδυνος	epikindhinos
dark	σκοτεινός	skotinos
date *calendar*	ἡμερομηνία	imerominia
daughter	κόρη	kori
day	μέρα	mera
dead	νεκρός	nekros

deaf	κουφός	koufos
dear	ἀγαπητός	aghapitos
December	Δεκέμβριος	dhekemvrios
deckchair	chaise longue	
declare (to)	δηλώνω	dhilono
deep	βαθύς	vathis
delay	ἀργοπορεία	arghoporia
deliver (to)	παραδίδω	paradhidho
delivery	διανομή	dhianomi
dentist	ὀδοντογιατρός	odhontoghiatros
deodorant	ἀποσμητικό γιά τόν ἱδρώτα	aposmitiko ghia ton idhrota
depart (to)	ἀναχωρῶ	anahoro
department	τμῆμα	tmima
department store	κατάστημα	katastima
departure	ἀναχώρηση	anahorissi
detour	στροφή πρός ἀποφυγήν ἐμποδίου	strofi pros apofighin embodhiou
develop (to) *film*	ἐμφανίζω	emfanizo
diamond	διαμάντι	dhiamandi
dictionary	λεξικό	lexiko
diet	δίαιτα	dhieta
diet (to)	κάνω δίαιτα	kano dhieta

different	διαφορετικός	dhiaforetikos
difficult	δύσκολος	dhiskolos
dine (to)	γευματίζω	ghevmatizo
dining room	τραπεζαρία	trapezaria
dinner	δεῖπνο	dhipno
direction	κατεύθυνση	katefthinssi
dirty	βρώμικος	vromikos
discotheque	discotheque	
dish	πιάτο	piato
disinfectant	ἀπολυμαντικό	apolimantiko
distance	ἀπόσταση	apostassi
disturb (to)	ἀνησυχῶ	anissiho
dive (to)	βουτῶ	vouto
diving board	ἐξέδρα γιά βουτιές	exedhra ghia vouties
divorced	χωρισμένος	horismenos
dizzy	ζαλισμένος	zalismenos
do (to)	κάνω	kano
dock (to)	πλευρίζω	plevrizo
doctor	γιατρός	ghiatros
dog	σκύλος	skilos
doll	κούκλα	koukla
dollar	δολλάριο	dholario
door	πόρτα	porta

double	διπλός	dhiplos
double bed	διπλό κρεββάτι	dhiplo krevati
double room	διπλό δωμάτιο	dhiplo dhomatio
down(stairs)	κάτω	kato
dozen	δώδεκα	dhodheka
drawer	συρτάρι	sirtari
dress	φόρεμα	forema
dressmaker	ράφτρα	raftra
drink (to)	πίνω	pino
drinking water	πόσιμο νερό	possimo nero
drive (to)	δηγῶ	odhigho
driver	δηγός	odhighos
driving licence	ἄδεια ὁδηγήσεως	adhia odhighisseos
dry	στεγνός	steghnos
dry cleaner	καθαριστήριο	katharistirio
duck	πάπια	papia
during	κατά τή διάρκεια	kata ti dhiarkia

E

each	κάθε	kathe
ear	αὐτί	afti
earache	πόνος αὐτιοῦ	ponos aftiou
early	νωρίς	noris

earrings	σκουλαρίκια	skoularikia
east	ἀνατολή	anatoli
Easter	Πάσχα	paskha
easy	εὔκολος	efkolos
eat (to)	τρώγω	trogho
egg	αὐγό	avgho
elastic	ἐλαστικός	elastikos
elbow	ἀγγώνας	angonas
electric light bulb	ἠλεκτρική λάμπα	ilektriki lamba
electric point	πρίζα	priza
elevator	ἀσανσέρ	assanser
embassy	πρεσβεία	presvia
emergency exit	ἔξοδος κινδύνου	exodhos kindhinou
empty	ἄδειος	adhios
end	τέλος	telos
engine	μηχανή	mihani
England	Ἀγγλία	anglia
English	Ἄγγλος	anglos
enlargement	μεγέθυνση	meghethinssi
enough	ἀρκετά	arketa
enquiries	πληροφορίες	plirofories
entrance	εἴσοδος	issodhos
envelope	φάκελλος	fakelos

equipment	ἐφόδιο	efodhio
Europe	Εὐρώπη	evropi
evening	βράδυ	vradhi
every	κάθε	kathe
everybody	ὅλοι	oli
everything	ὅλα	ola
everywhere	παντοῦ	pantou
example	παράδειγμα	paradhighma
except	ἐκτός	ektos
excess	ὑπερβολή	ipervoli
exchange *bureau*	τράπεζα	trapeza
exchange rate	τιμή συναλλάγματος	timi sinalaghmatos
excursion	ἐκδρομή	ekdhromi
exhibition	ἔκθεση	ekthessi
exit	ἔξοδος	exodhos
expect (to)	περιμένω	perimeno
expensive	ἀκριβός	akrivos
express	κατεπεῖγον	katepighon
express train	ταχεία	tahia
eye	μάτι	mati
eye shadow	μακιγιάζ ματιῶν	makighiaz mation

F

| face | πρόσωπο | prossopo |

face cream	καλλυντική κρέμα	kalintiki krema
face powder	πούδρα	poudhra
factory	ἐργοστάσιο	erghostassio
faint (to)	λιποθυμῶ	lipothimo
fair *colour*	ξανθός	ksanthos
fall (to)	πέφτω	pefto
family	οἰκογένεια	ikoghenia
far	μακρυά	makria
fare	εἰσιτήριο	issitirio
farm	κτῆμα	ktima
farther	πιό μακριά	pio makria
fashion	μόδα	modha
fast	γρήγορα	ghrighora
fat	παχύς	pahis
father	πατέρας	pateras
fault	λάθος	lathos
February	Φεβρουάριος	fevrouarios
feel (to)	αἰσθάνομαι	esthanome
ferry	ferry-boat	
fetch (to)	φέρνω	ferno
a few	λίγα	ligha
field	ἀγρός	aghros
fig	σῦκο	siko

fill (to)	γεμίζω	ghemizo
film	film	
find (to)	βρίσκω	vrisko
fine	πρόστιμο	prostimo
finger	δάκτυλο	dhaktilo
finish (to)	τελειώνω	teliono
finished	τελειωμένος	teliomenos
fire	φωτιά	fotia
first	πρῶτος	protos
first class	πρώτη θέση	proti thessi
fish	ψάρι	psari
fish (to)	ψαρεύω	psarevo
fisherman	ψαρᾶς	psaras
fishmonger	ψαρᾶς	psaras
fit (to)	χωρῶ	horo
flag	σημαία	simea
flat	διαμέρισμα	dhiamerisma
flat	ἐπίπεδος	epipedhos
flight	πτήση	ptissi
flint *lighter*	πέτρα ἀναπτήρα	petra anaptira
flood	πλημμύρα	plimira
floor	πάτωμα	patoma
floor show	παράσταση	parastassi

florist	ἀνθοπώλης	anthopolis
flower	λουλούδι	louloudhi
fly	μῦγα	migha
fly (to)	πετῶ	peto
follow (to)	ἀκολουθῶ	akoloutho
food	φαΐ	fai
foot	πόδι	podhi
football	ποδόσφαιρο	podhosfero
footpath	μονοπάτι	monopati
for	γιά	ghia
forehead	μέτωπο	metopo
forest	δάσος	dhassos
forget (to)	ξεχνῶ	ksehno
fork	πειρούνι	pirouni
forward	μπρός	bros
forward (to)	πρός τά μπρός	pros ta bros
fracture	σπάσιμο	spassimo
fragile	εὔθραυστος	efthrafstos
free	ἐλεύθερος	eleftheros
fresh	φρέσκος	freskos
fresh water	φρέσκο νερό	fresko nero
Friday	Παρασκευή	paraskevi
friend	φίλος	filos

from	ἀπό	apo
front	μπρός	bros
frontier	σύνορο	sinoro
frozen	παγωμένος	paghomenos
fruit	φροῦτο	fruto
fruiterer	φρουτᾶς, ὀπωροπώλης	froutas, oporopolis
fruit juice	χυμός φρούτων	himos frouton
full	γεμᾶτος	ghematos
full board	μέ ὅλα τά γεύματα	me ola ta ghevmata
funny	ἀστεῖος	astios
fur	γούνα	ghouna

G

gallery	αἴθουσα ἐκθέσεων	ethussa ekthesseon
gamble (to)	χαρτοπαίζω	hartopezo
game	παιγνίδι	peghnidhi
garage	γκαράζ	garaz
garden	κῆπος	kipos
garlic	σκόρδο	skordho
gas	γκάζι	gazi
gate	πόρτα	porta
gentlemen	κύριος	kirios

get (to)	πηγαίνω	pigheno
get off (to)	βγαίνω	vgheno
get on (to)	ἀνεβαίνω	aneveno
gift	δῶρο	dhoro
girdle	ζώνη	zoni
girl	κορίτσι	koritsi
give (to)	δίνω	dhino
glad	εὐχαριστημένος	efharistimenos
glass	ποτήρι	potiri
glasses	γυαλιά	ghialia
glove	γάντι	ghanti
go (to)	πηγαίνω	pigheno
God	Θεός	theos
gold	χρυσός	hrissos
good	καλός	kalos
good-bye	χαίρετε	herete
good day, morning	καλημέρα	kalimera
good evening	καλησπέρα	kalispera
good night	καληνύκτα	kalinikta
government	κυβέρνηση	kivernissi
granddaughter	ἐγγονή	engoni
grandfather	παππούς	papous
grandmother	γιαγιά	ghiaghia

grandson	ἔγγονός	engonos
grape	σταφύλι	stafili
grass	γρασίδι	ghrassidhi
grateful	εὐγνώμων	evghnomon
great	μεγάλος	meghalos
Greece	Ἑλλάδα	eladha
Greek *adj.*	Ἑλληνικός	elinikos
green	πράσινος	prassinos
greengrocer	λαχανοπώλης	lahanopolis
grey	γκρίζος	grizos
grocer	μπακάλης	bakalis
guarantee	ἐγγύηση	englissi
guest	ἐπισκέπτης	episkeptis
guide	ὁδηγός	odhighos
guide book	τουριστικός ὁδηγός	touristikos odhighos

H

hair	μαλλιά	malia
hair brush	βούρτσα μαλλιῶν	vourtsa malion
haircut	κούρεμα	kourema
hairdresser	κουρέας	koureas
hairpin	φουρκέτα	fourketa
half	μισός	missos

half fare	μισό εισιτήριο	misso issitirio
hand	χέρι	heri
handbag	τσάντα	tsanta
handkerchief	μαντήλι	mandili
hanger	κρεμάστρα	kremastra
happen (to)	συμβαίνω	simveno
happy	εὐτυχισμένος	eftihismenos
harbour	λιμάνι	limani
hard	σκληρός	skliros
hat	καπέλλο	kapelo
have (to)	ἔχω	eho
he	αὐτός	aftos
head	κεφάλι	kefali
headache	πονοκέφαλος	ponokefalos
headwaiter	ἀρχισερβιτόρος	arhiservitoros
health	ὑγεία	ighia
hear (to)	ἀκούω	akouo
heart	καρδιά	kardhia
heat	ζέστη	zesti
heating	θέρμανση	thermanssi
heavy	βαρύς	varis
heel *foot*	φτέρνα	fterna
heel *shoe*	τακούνι	takouni

help	βοήθεια	voithia
help (to)	βοηθῶ	voitho
her *pron.*	αὐτήν	aftin
here	ἐδῶ	edho
high	ψηλά	psila
hill	λόφος	lofos
him	αὐτόν	afton
hip	ἰσχίον	ishion
hire (to)	νοικιάζω	nikiazo
hitch hike (to)	ὀτοστόπ	autostop
holiday	γιορτή	ghiorti
(at) home	στό σπίτι	sto spiti
honey	μέλι	meli
horse	ἄλογο	alogho
horse races	ἱπποδρομίες	ipodhromies
hospital	νοσοκομεῖο	nossokomio
hot	ζεστός	zestos
hotel	ξενοδοχεῖο	xenodhohio
hotel keeper	ξενοδόχος	xenodhohos
hot water bottle	μπουγιότα	boughiota
hour	ὥρα	ora
house	σπίτι	spiti
how ?	πῶς;	pos

how much, many ?	πόσα	possa
hungry (to be)	πεινάω	pinao
hurry (to)	βιάζομαι	viazome
hurt (to)	βλάπτω	vlapto
husband	άνδρας, σύζυγος	andhras, sizighos

I

I	ἐγώ	egho
ice	πάγος	paghos
ice cream	παγωτό	paghoto
if	ἄν	ahn
ill	ἄρρωστος	arostos
illness	ἀρρώστια	arostia
immediately	ἀμέσως	amessos
important	σπουδαῖος	spoudheos
in	μέσα	messa
include	συμπεριλαμβάνω	simberilamvano
included	συμπεριλαμβανόμενο	simberilamvanomeno
inconvenient	ἄβολος	avolos
incorrect	λανθασμένος	lanthasmenos
indigestion	δυσπεψία	dhispepsia
information	πληροφορία	pliroforia
ink	μελάνι	melani

inn	χάνι	hani
insect	ἔντομο	endomo
insect bite	τσίμπημα ἀπό ἔντομο	tsimbima apo endomo
insect repellent	λοσιόν γιά τήν ἀπώθηση ἐντόμων	lossion ghia tin apothissi entomon
inside	μέσα	messa
instead	ἀντί	andi
insurance	ἀσφάλεια	asfalia
insure (to)	ἀσφαλίζω	asfalizo
interesting	ἐνδιαφέρον	endhiaferon
interpreter	μεταφραστής, διερμηνέας	metafrastis, dhiermineas
into	μέσα	messa
introduce (to)	συστήνω	sistino
invitation	πρόσκληση	prosklissi
invite (to)	προσκαλῶ	proskalo
Ireland	'Ιρλανδία	irlandhia
Irish	'Ιρλανδός	irlandhos
iron (to)	σιδερώνω	sidherono
island	νησί	nissi
it	αὐτό	afto

J

| jacket | σακκάκι | sakaki |

jam	μαρμελάδα	marmeladha
January	Ἰανουάριος	ianouarios
jar	βάζο	vazo
jaw	μασέλα	massela
jelly fish	τσούχτρα	tsouhtra
jeweller	ἀδαμαντοπώλης	adhamandopolis
jewellery	διαμαντικά	dhiamandika
journey	ταξίδι	taxidhi
juice	χυμός	himos
July	Ἰούλιος	ioulios
jumper	pullover	
June	Ἰούνιος	iounios

K

keep (to)	κρατῶ	krato
key	κλειδί	klidhi
kind	εἶδος	idhos
king	βασιλιᾶς	vassilias
kitchen	κουζίνα	kouzina
knee	γόνατο	ghonato
knickers/briefs	κιλότες/σώβρακα	kilotes/sovraka
knife	μαχαῖρι	maheri
know (to) *fact*	γνωρίζω	ghnorizo

know (to) *person*	ξέρω	ksero

L

label	ταμπέλα	tabela
lace	δαντέλα	dhantela
ladies	κυρίες	kiries
lake	λίμνη	limni
lamp	λάμπα	lamba
landlord	ιδιοκτήτης	idhioktitis
lane	λουρίδα δρόμου	louridha dhromou
language	γλῶσσα	ghlossa
large	μεγάλος	meghalos
last	τελευταῖος	telefteos
late	ἀργά	argha
laugh (to)	γελῶ	ghelo
laundry	πλυντήριο	plindirio
lavatory	ἀποχωρητήριο	apohoritirio
lavatory paper	χαρτί τουαλέτας	harti toualetas
law	νόμος	nomos
laxative	καθαρκτικό	katharktiko
lead (to)	ὁδηγῶ	odhigho
learn (to)	μαθαίνω	matheno
leather	δέρμα	dherma

leave (to) *abandon*	ἐγκαταλείπω	engatalipo
leave (to) *go away*	φεύγω	fevgho
left	ἀριστερά	aristera
left luggage	ἀποσκευές	aposkeves
leg	πόδι	podhi
lemon	λεμόνι	lemoni
lemonade	λεμονάδα	lemonadha
lend (to)	δανείζω	dhanizo
length	μῆκος	mikos
less	λιγότερο	lighotero
let (to) *rent*	νοικιάζω	nikiazo
let (to) *allow*	ἐπιτρέπω	epitrepo
letter	γράμμα	ghrama
lettuce	μαρούλι	marouli
library	βιβλιοθήκη	vivliothiki
licence	ἄδεια	adhia
life	ζωή	zoi
lift	ἀσανσέρ	assansser
light *illumination*	φῶς	fos
light *weight*	ἐλαφρύς	elafris
lighter fuel	βενζίνη ἀναπτῆρος	venzini anaptiros
lighthouse	φάρος	faros
like (to) *it pleases me*	μοῦ ἀρέσει	mou aressi

like (to) *wish*	θέλω	thelo
linen	λινό	lino
lip	χείλος	hilos
lipstick	κραγιόν	kraghion
listen	ἀκούω	akouo
little *amount*	λίγος	lighos
little *size*	μικρός	mikros
live (to)	ζῶ	zo
loaf	φραντζόλα	frandzola
local	ντόπιο	dopio
lock	κλειδαριά	klidharia
long	μακρύς	makris
look (to)	βλέπω	vlepo
look (to) *seem*	φαίνομαι	fenome
look for (to)	ψάχνω	psahno
lorry	φορτηγό	fortigho
lose (to)	χάνω	hano
lost property office	γραφείο χαμένων ἀντικειμένων	ghrafio hamenon antikimenon
loud	δυνατά	dhinata
lovely	ὅμορφος	omorfos
low	χαμηλός	hamilos
luggage	ἀποσκευές	aposkeves

lunch	μεσημεριανό φαγητό	messimeriano faghito
M		
magazine	περιοδικό	periodhiko
maid	υπηρέτρια	ipiretria
mail	ταχυδρομείο	tahidhromio
main street	κύριος δρόμος	kirios dhromos
make (to)	κάνω	kano
make-up	μακιγιάζ	makighiaz
man	άνδρας	andhras
manager	διευθυντής	dhiefthindis
manicure	μανικιούρ	manicure
many	πολλοί	poli
map	χάρτης	hartis
March	Μάρτιος	martios
market	αγορά	aghora
marmalade	μαρμελάδα	marmeladha
married	παντρεμένος	pandremenos
match	σπίρτο	spirto
match *sport*	match	
material	υλικό	iliko
mattress	στρώμα	stroma
May	Μάιος	maios

me	ἐμένα	emena
meal	γεῦμα	ghevma
measurements	μέτρα	metra
meat	κρέας	kreas
medicine	φάρμακο	farmako
meet (to)	συναντῶ	sinanto
melon	πεπόνι	peponi
mend (to)	ἐπιδιορθώνω	epidhiorthono
menu	menu	
message	μήνυμα	minima
metal	μέταλλο	metalo
midday	μεσημέρι	messimeri
middle	μέσος	messos
midnight	μεσάνυκτα	messanikta
mild	ἤπιος	ipios
milk	γάλα	ghala
mineral water	μεταλλικό νερό	metaliko nero
minute	λεπτό	lepto
mirror	καθρέπτης	kathreptis
Miss	δεσποινής	dhespinis
miss (to) *train, etc.*	χάνω	hano
mistake	λάθος	lathos
modern	μοντέρνος	modernos

moment	στιγμή	stighmi
monastery	μοναστήρι	monastiri
Monday	Δευτέρα	dheftera
money	χρήματα, λεπτά	hrimata, lepta
money order	χρηματική ἐπιταγή	hrimatiki epitaghi
month	μήνας	minas
monument	μνημεῖο	mnimio
more	περισσότερο	perissotero
morning	πρωί	proï
mosquito	κουνούπι	kounoupi
mother	μητέρα	mitera
motor	μηχανή	mihani
motor boat	βενζινάκατος	venzinakatos
motor cycle	μοτοσυκλέτα	motossikleta
motorway	αὐτοκινητόδρομος	aftokinitodhromos
mountain	βουνό	vouno
mouth	στόμα	stoma
Mr	κύριος	kirios
Mrs	κυρία	kiria
much	πολύ	poli
museum	μουσεῖο	moussio
mushroom	μανιτάρι	manitari
music	μουσική	moussiki

mustard	μουστάρδα	moustardha
my, mine	μου, δικό μου	mou, dhiko mou

N

nail *finger*	νύχι	nihi
nailbrush	βούρτσα νυχιών	vourtsa nihion
nailfile	λίμα νυχιών	lima nihion
name	όνομα	onoma
napkin	πετσέτα	petseta
nappy	πάνα μωρού	pana morou
narrow	στενός	stenos
near	κοντά	konda
necessary	άναγκαῖο	anangeo
neck	λαιμός	lemos
necklace	κολιέ	kolie
need (to)	χρειάζομαι	hriazome
needle	βελόνα	velona
never	ποτέ	pote
new	καινούργιο	kenourghio
news	είδήσεις	idhissis
newsagaent	έφημεριδοπωλεῖο	efimeridhopolio
newspaper	έφημερίδα	efimeridha
next	έπόμενος	epomenos

nice	ὡραῖος	oreos
night	νύκτα	nikta
nightclub	κέντρο διασκεδάσεως	kendro dhiaskedhasseos
nightdress	νυκτικό	niktiko
no	ὄχι	ohi
nobody	κανείς	kanis
noisy	θορυβώδης	thorivodhis
none	κανένας	kanenas
north	βορρᾶς	voras
nose	μύτη	miti
not	δέν, μή	dhen, mi
note	νότα	nota
notebook	τετράδιο	tetradhio
nothing	τίποτα	tipota
notice	εἰδοποίηση	idhopiissi
notice (to)	παρατηρῶ	paratiro
novel	μυθιστόρημα	mithistorima
November	Νοέμβριος	noemvrios
number	ἀριθμός	arithmos
nurse	νοσοκόμα	nossokoma
nut	καρύδι	karidhi
nylon	nylon	

O

occupied	κατειλημμένος	katilimenos
ocean	ὠκεανός	okeanos
October	᾽Οκτώβριος	oktovrios
odd *strange*	παράξενος	paraxenos
of	ἀπό	apo
office	γραφεῖο	ghrafio
official	ἐπίσημος	epissimos
often	συχνά	sihna
oil	λάδι	ladhi
ointment	ἀλοιφή	alifi
old	γέρος, παλιός	gheros, palios
olive	ἐλhά	elia
on	πάνω	pano
once	μιά φορά	mia fora
only	μόνο	mono
open (to)	ἀνοίγω	anigho
open *pp., adj.*	ἄνοιξε	anixe
opera	opera	
operation	ἐγχείρηση	enhirissi
opposite	ἀντίθετος	antithetos
optician	ὀφθαλμίατρος	ofthalmiatros
or	ἤ	i

orange	πορτοκάλι	portokali
orchestra	ὀρχήστρα	orhistra
order (to)	διατάζω	dhiatazo
ordinary	συνηθισμένος	sinithismenos
orthodox	ὀρθόδοξος	orthodhoxos
other	ἄλλος	alos
our, ours	μας, δικός μας	mas, dhikos mas
out(side)	ἔξω	exo
out of order	χαλασμένος	halasmenos
over	ἀπό πάνω	apo pano
overcoat	παλτό	palto
over there	ἐκεῖ	eki
owe (to)	χρωστῶ	hrosto
owner	ἰδιοκτήτης	idhioktitis

P

pack (to)	πακετάρω	paketaro
packet	πακέτο	paketo
page	σελίδα	selidha
paid	πληρωμένος	pliromenos
pain	πόνος	ponos
paint (to)	ζωγραφίζω	zoghrafizo
painting	πίνακας ζωγραφικῆς	pinakas zoghrafikis

pair	ζευγάρι	zevghari
palace	παλάτι	palati
pale	χλωμός	hlomos
paper	χαρτί	harti
paraffin	παραφίνη, πετρέλαιο	parafini, petreleo
parcel	πακέτο	paketo
park (to)	σταθμεύω	stathmevo
park	πάρκο	parko
part	μέρος	meros
parting *hair*	χωρίστρα	horistra
pass (to)	περνῶ	perno
passenger	ἐπιβάτης	epivatis
passport	διαβατήριο	dhiavatirio
path	μονοπάτι	monopati
patient *adj.*	ὑπομον ετικός	ipomon etikos
pavement	πεζοδρόμιο	pezodhromio
pay (to)	πληρώνω	plirono
peach	ροδάκινο	rodhakino
pear	ἀχλάδι	ahladhi
pearl	πέρλα, μαργαριτάρι	perla, margharitari
peas	μπιζέλια	bizelia
pedestrian	πεζός	pezos

pen	πέννα	pena
(fountain) pen	στυλό	stilo
pencil	μολύβι	molivi
penknife	σουγιᾶς	soughias
people	κόσμος	kosmos
pepper	πιπέρι	piperi
performance	παράσταση	parastassi
perfume	ἄρωμα	aroma
perhaps	ἴσως	issos
perishable	φθαρτό	ftharto
perm	περμανάντ	permanant
permit	ἄδεια	adhia
permit (to)	ἐπιτρέπω	epitrepo
person	ἄνθρωπος	anthropos
personal	προσωπικός	prossopikos
petrol	βενζίνη	venzini
petrol can	δοχεῖο βενζίνης	dhohio venzinis
petrol station	σταθμός βενζίνης	stathmos venzinis
photograph	φωτογραφία	fotoghrafia
photographer	φωτογράφος	fotoghrafos
piano	πιάνο	piano
picnic	picnic	
piece	κομμάτι	komati

pillow	μαξιλάρι	maxilari
pin	βελόνα	velona
(safety) pin	παραμάνα	paramana
pineapple	ἀνανάς	ananas
pink	ρόζ	roz
pipe	πίπα	pipa
place	μέρος	meros
plain	ἁπλός	aplos
plan	σχέδιο	skhedhio
(adhesive) plaster	λευκοπλάστης	lefkoplastis
plastic	πλαστικός	plastikos
plate	πιάτο	piato
platform	ἐξέδρα	exedhra
play (to)	παίζω	pezo
play	παιγνίδι	peghnidhi
please	παρακαλῶ	parakalo
plug *electric*	πρίζα	priza
plug *bath*	βούλωμα	vouloma
plum	δαμάσκηνο	dhamaskino
pocket	τσέπη	tsepi
point	σημεῖο	simmio
poisonous	δηλητηριώδης	dhilitiriodhis
policeman	ἀστυνόμος	astinomos

police station	ἀστυνομία	astinomia
poor	φτωχός	ftohos
pope	πάπας	papas
popular	δημοφιλής	dhimofilis
port	λιμάνι	limani
porter	θυρωρός	thiroros
possible	δυνατόν	dhinaton
post (to)	ταχυδρομῶ	tahidhromo
post box	ταχυδρομικό κυβώτιο	tahidhromiko kivotio
postcard	κάρτ ποστάλ	carte postale
postman	ταχυδρόμος	tahidhromos
post office	ταχυδρομεῖο	tahidhromio
poste restante	poste restante	
potato	πατάτα	patata
pound	λίρα	lira
powder	σκόνη	skoni
prefer (to)	προτιμῶ	protimo
prepare (to)	ἑτοιμάζω	etimazo
prescription	συνταγή	sintaghi
present *gift*	δῶρο	dhoro
press (to)	σιδερώνω	sidherono
pretty *fem.*	ὄμορφη	omorfi
price	τιμή	timi

private	ιδιωτικός	idhiotikos
problem	πρόβλημα	provlima
profession	επάγγελμα	epangelma
programme	πρόγραμμα	proghramma
promise (to)	υπόσχομαι	iposkhome
pull (to)	τραβώ	travo
pure	γνήσιο	ghnissio
purse	πορτοφόλι	portofoli
push (to)	σκουντώ	skoundo
put (to)	βάζω	vazo
pyjamas	πιτζάμες	pitzames

Q

quality	ποιότητα	piotita
quantity	ποσότητα	possotita
quarter	τέταρτο	tetarto
queen	βασίλισσα	vassilissa
question	ερώτηση	erotissi
quick	γρήγορος	ghrighoros
quiet	ήσυχος	issihos

R

| racecourse | ιπποδρόμιο | ipodhromio |
| race | αγώνας δρόμου | aghonas dhromou |

radiator	καλοριφέρ	kalorifer
radio	ραδιόφωνο	radhiofono
railway	σιδηρόδρομος	sidhirodhromos
rain	βροχή	vrohi
(it is) raining	βρέχει	vrehi
raincoat	ἀδιάβροχο	adhiavroho
rare	σπάνιος	spanios
raw	ὠμός	omos
razor	ξυράφι	ksirafi
razor blade	ξυραφάκι	ksirafaki
read (to)	διαβάζω	dhiavazo
ready	ἕτοιμος	etimos
real	πραγματικός	praghmatikos
really	πραγματικά	praghmatika
reason	λογική	loghiki
receipt	ἀπόδειξη	apodhixi
receive (to)	λαβαίνω	laveno
recent	πρόσφατος	prosfatos
recommend	συστήνω	sistino
record	δίσκος γραμμοφώνου	dhiskos ghramofonou
red	κόκκινος	kokinos
refreshments	ἀναψυκτικά	anapsiktika
register (to)	δηλώνω	dhilono

registered mail	συστημένο γράμμα	sistimeno ghrama
remember (to)	θυμᾶμαι	thimame
rent (to)	νοικιάζω	nikiazo
repair (to)	διορθώνω	dhiorthono
repeat (to)	ἐπαναλαμβάνω	epanalamvano
reply (to)	ἀπαντῶ	apanto
reply paid	πληρωμένη ἀπάντηση	pliromeni apantissi
reservation	κράτηση	kratissi
reserve (to)	κρατῶ, κλείνω	krato, klino
reserved	κλεισμένο	klismeno
restaurant	ἐστιατόριο	estiatorio
restaurant car	wagon restaurant	
return (to)	ἐπιστρέφω	epistrefo
rib	πλευρό	plevro
ribbon	κορδέλλα	kordhela
rice	ρίζι	rizi
right *opp. left*	δεξιός	dhexios
right *opp. wrong*	ὀρθός	orthos
ring	δακτυλίδι	dhaktilidhi
river	ποταμός	potamos
road	δρόμος	dhromos
rock	βράχος	vrahos
roll *bread*	ψωμάκι	psomaki

room	δωμάτιο	dhomatio
rope	σκοινί	skini
round	γύρω	ghiro
rowing boat	βάρκα	varka
rubber	λάστιχο	lastiho
rubbish	σκουπίδια	skoupidhia
run (to)	τρέχω	treho
Russia	Ρωσσία	rossia
Russian	Ρῶσσος	rossos

S

safe	ἀσφαλής	asfalis
salad	σαλάτα	salata
salesgirl	πωλήτρια	politria
salesman	πωλητής	politis
salt	ἁλάτι	alati
salt water	ἁλμυρό νερό	almiro nero
same	ἴδιος	idhios
sand	ἄμμος	amos
sandals	σανδάλια	sandhalia
sandwich	sandwich	
sanitary towel	πετσέτα ὑγείας	petseta ighias
Saturday	Σάββατο	savato

sauce	σάλτσα	saltsa
saucer	πιατάκι	piataki
sausage	λουκάνικο	loukaniko
say (to)	λέω	leo
scald (to)	ζεματίζω	zematizo
scarf	σάλι	sali
scent	άρωμα	aroma
school	σχολείο	skholio
scissors	ψαλίδι	psalidhi
Scotland	Σκωτία	skotia
Scottish	Σκωτσέζικο	skotseziko
sculpture	γλυπτική	ghliptiki
sea	θάλασσα	thalassa
seasick	έχω ναυτία	eho naftia
season	εποχή	epohi
seat	θέση	thessi
second	δεύτερος	dhefteros
second class	δεύτερη θέση	dhefteri thessi
sedative	καταπραϋντικό	katapraintiko
see (to)	βλέπω	vlepo
seem (to)	φαίνομαι	fenome
sell (to)	πουλώ	poulo
send (to)	στέλνω	stelno

separate	χωριστός	horistos
September	Σεπτέμβριος	septemvrios
serious	σοβαρός	sovaros
serve (to)	σερβίρω	serviro
service	υπηρεσία	ipiressia
service charge	ποσοστό σερβιτόρου	possosto servitorou
set *hair*	μιζαμπλί	mizampli
several	αρκετός	arketos
sew (to)	ράβω	ravo
shade *colour*	απόχρωση	apohrossi
shade *shadow*	σκιά	skia
shallow	ρηχός	rihos
shampoo	shampoo	
shape	σχῆμα	skhima
share (to)	μοιράζομαι	mirazome
sharp	οξύς, κοφτερός	oxis, kofteros
shave (to)	ξυρίζομαι	ksirizome
shaving brush	βούρτσα ξυρίσματος	vourtsa ksirismatos
shaving cream	κρέμα ξυρίσματος	krema ksirismatos
she	αυτή	afti
sheet	σεντόνι	sendoni
shell	κέλυφος, κοχύλι	kelifos, kohili
shine (to)	γυαλίζω	ghializo

shingle	βότσαλο	votsalo
ship	καράβι ,πλοῖο	karavi, plio
shipping line	ναυτιλιακή γραμμή	naftiliaki ghrami
shirt	πουκάμισο	poukamisso
shoe	παπούτσι	papoutsi
shoelace	κορδόνι παπουτσιῶν	kordhoni papoutsion
shoe shop	ὑποδηματοπωλεῖο	ipodhimatopolio
shoe repairs	τσαγγαράδικο	tsangaradhiko
shop	κατάστημα, μαγαζί	katastima, maghazi
short	κοντός	kondos
shorts	shorts	
shoulder	ὦμος	omos
show	παράσταση	parastassi
show (to)	δείχνω	dhihno
shower	ντούς	douche
shut	κλείνω	klino
sick	ἄρρωστος	arostos
side	πλευρά	plevra
sightseeing	ἐπίσκεψη τῶν ἀξιοθεάτων	episkepsi ton axiotheaton
sights	ἀξιοθέατα	axiotheata
silk	μετάξι	metaxi
silver	ἀσημένιος	assimenios

simple	ἁπλός	aplos
single	μονός	monos
single room	μονό δωμάτιο	mono dhomatio
sister	ἀδελφή	adhelfi
sit (to)	κάθομαι	kathome
sit down (to)	κάθομαι κάτω	kathome kato
size	μέγεθος	meghethos
ski (to)	κάνω σκί	kano ski
skid (to)	γλιστρῶ	ghlistro
sky	οὐρανός	ouranos
sleep (to)	κοιμᾶμαι	kimame
sleeper	wagon lit	
sleeping bag	sleeping bag	
sleeve	μανίκι	maniki
slice	φέτα	feta
slip	μισοφόρι, κομπινεζόν	missofori, combinezon
slippers	παντοῦφλες	pandoufles
slowly	ἀργά	argha
small	μικρός	mikros
smart	κομψός	kompsos
smell (to)	μυρίζω	mirizo
smoke (to)	καπνίζω	kapnizo

smoking (compartment)	καπνιστήριο	kapnistirio
(no) smoking	ἀπαγορεύεται τό κάπνισμα	apaghorevete to kapnisma
snack	μεζές	mezes
snow	χιόνι	hioni
(it is) snowing	χιονίζει	hionizi
so	ἔτσι	etsi
soap	σαπούνι	sapouni
soap powder	σκόνη σαπουνιοῦ	skoni sapouniou
sock	κάλτσα	kaltsa
soda water	σόδα	sodha
sold	πουλημένο	poulimeno
sole *shoe*	σόλα	sola
some	λίγο	ligho
somebody	κάποιος	kapios
something	κάτι	kati
sometimes	μερικές φορές	merikes fores
somewhere	κάπου	kapou
son	γιός	ghios
song	τραγούδι	traghoudhi
soon	γρήγορα	ghrighora
sorry	συγγνώμη	sighnomi

soup	σούπα	soupa
sour	ξινός	ksinos
south	νότος	notos
souvenir	ἐνθύμιο	enthimio
speak (to)	μιλῶ	milo
speciality	εἰδικότητα	idhikotita
speed	ταχύτητα	tahitita
speed limit	ὅριον ταχύτητος	orion tahititos
spend (to)	ξοδεύω	ksodhevo
spine	σπονδυλική στήλη	spondhiliki stili
spoon	κουτάλι	koutali
sport	παιγνίδι	peghnidhi
sprain	στραγγούλισμα	strangoulisma
sprain (to)	στραγγουλίζω	stangoulizo
spring *season*	ἄνοιξη	anixi
square *shape*	τετράγωνος	tetraghonos
square *in city*	πλατεία	platia
stage	σκηνή	skini
stain	λεκές	lekes
stained	λεκιασμένος	lekiasmenos
stairs	σκάλες	skales
stale	μπαγιάτικος	baghiatikos
stalls	πλατεία	platia

stamp	γραμματόσημο	ghramatossimo
stand (to)	στέκομαι	stekome
start (to)	ξεκινῶ	ksekino
station	σταθμός	stathmos
stationer	χαρτοπώλης	hartopolis
statue	ἄγαλμα	aghalma
stay (to)	μένω	meno
step	βῆμα	vima
still *not moving*	ἀκίνητος	akinitos
sting	τσιμπῶ	tsimbo
stocking	κάλτσα	kaltsa
stolen	κλεμμένο	klemeno
stomach	στομάχι	stomahi
stone	πέτρα	petra
stop (to)	σταματῶ	stamato
store	κατάστημα	katastima
straight	ἴσια	issia
straight on	ἴσια μπρός	issia bros
strap	λουρί	louri
strawberry	φράουλα	fraoula
stream	ρυάκι	riaki
street	δρόμος	dhromos
string	σπάγγος	spangos

strong	δυνατός	dhinatos
student	μαθητής, φοιτητής	mathitis, fititis
style	στύλ	still
suburb	περίχωρο	perihoro
subway	υπόγειος	ipoghios
suede	suede	
sugar	ζάχαρη	zahari
suit	φορεσιά	foressia
suitcase	βαλίτσα	valitsa
summer	καλοκαίρι	kalokeri
sun	ήλιος	ilios
sunbathing	ηλιοθεραπεία	iliotherapia
sunburn	ηλιόκαμα	iliokama
Sunday	Κυριακή	kiriaki
sunglasses	γυαλιά ήλιου	ghialia iliou
sunhat	καπέλλο ήλιου	kapelo iliou
sunshade	ομπρέλλα ήλιου	ombrella iliou
sunstroke	ηλίαση	iliassi
suntan cream	κρέμα ήλιου	krema iliou
supper	δείπνο	dhipno
supplementary charge	πρόσθετη χρέωση	prostheti hreossi
sure	βέβαιος	veveos
surface mail	κοινό γράμμα	kino ghrama

surgery	χειρουργείο	hirourghio
suspender belt	τιράντες	tirandes
sweater	pullover	
sweet	γλυκός	ghlikos
sweets	γλυκά	ghlika
swell (to)	πρήζομαι	prizome
swim (to)	κολυμπῶ	kolimbo
swimming pool	πισίνα	pissina
switch *light*	διακόπτης	dhiakoptis
swollen	πρησμένος	prismenos

T

table	τραπέζι	trapezi
tablecloth	τραμεζομάνδυλο	trapezomandhilo
tablet	χάπι	hapi
tailor	ράφτης	raftis
take (to)	παίρνω	perno
talk (to)	μιλῶ	milo
tall	ψηλός	psilos
tap	βρύση	vrissi
taste	γεύση	ghefssi
tax	φόρος	foros
taxi	ταξί	taxi

tea	τσάι	tsaï
teach (to)	διδάσκω	dhidhasko
telegram	τηλεγράφημα	tileghrafima
telephone (to)	τηλεφωνῶ	tilefono
telephone	τηλέφωνο	tilefono
telephone box	τηλεφωνικός θάλαμος	tilefonikos thalamos
telephone call	τηλεφώνημα	tilefonima
telephone directory	τηλεφωνικός κατάλογος	tilefonikos kataloghos
telephone number	τηλεφωνικός ἀριθμός	tilefonikos arithmos
telephone operator *male, female*	τηλεφωνητής, τηλεφωνήτρια	tilefonitis, tilefonitria
television	τηλεόραση	tileorassi
tell (to)	λέω	leo (-e pronounced as in let)
temperature	θερμοκρασία	thermokrassia
tent	τέντα	tenda
tent peg	παλούκι τέντας	palouki tendas
tent pole	πάσσαλος τέντας	passalos tendas
terrace	ταράτσα	taratsa
than	ἀπό	apo
thank you	εὐχαριστῶ	efharisto
that	ἐκεῖνο	ekino
the	τό	to (as in 'go')

theatre	θέατρο	theatro
their, theirs	τους, δικό τους	tous, dhiko tous
them	αὐτούς	aftous
then	τότε	tote
there	ἐκεῖ	eki
there is	εἶναι	ine
there are	εἶναι	ine
thermometer	θερμόμετρο	thermometro
these	αὐτά	afta
they	αὐτοί	afti
thick	πηκτός	piktos
thin	λεπτό	lepto
thing	πρᾶγμα	praghma
think (to)	σκέπτομαι	skeptome
thirsty (to be)	διψῶ	dhipso
this	αὐτό	afto
those	ἐκεῖνα	ekina
thread	κλωστή	klosti
throat	λαιμός	lemos
through	διά	dhia
throw (to)	πετῶ	peto
thumb	ἀντίχειρ	antihir
Thursday	Πέμπτη	pempti

ticket	εἰσιτήριο	issitirio
tide	παλίρροια	paliria
tie	γραβάτα	ghravata
tight	στενός	stenos
time	ὥρα	ora
timetable	ὡράριο	orario
tin	κονσέρβα	konserva
tin opener	ἀνοικτήρι κονσερβῶν	aniktiri konsservon
tip	ἄκρη	akri
tip (to)	δίνω φιλοδώρημα	dhino filodhorima
tired	κουρασμένος	kourasmenos
tissues *paper*	χαρτομάντηλα	hartomandila
to *place*	στό	sto
tobacco	καπνός	kapnos
tobacco pouch	καπνοσακκούλα	kapnosakoula
tobacconist	καπνοπώλης	kapnopolis
today	σήμερα	simera
toe	δάκτυλο ποδιοῦ	dhaktilo podhiou
together	μαζί	mazi
toilet	τουαλέτα, ἀποχωρητήριο	toualeta, apohoritirio
toilet paper	χαρτί ἀποχωρητήριου	harti apohoritiriou

token *telephone*	μάρκα	marka
tomato	ντομάτα	domata
tomorrow	αὔριο	avrio
tongue	γλῶσσα	ghlossa
tonight	ἀπόψε	apopse
too *excessive*	πάρα πολύ	para poli
too *also*	ἐπίσης	epissis
too much/many	πάρα πολύ/παρά πολλά	para poli/para pola
tooth	δόντι	dhonti
toothache	πονόδοντας	ponodhondas
toothbrush	ὀδοντόβουρτσα	odhontovourtsa
toothpaste	ὀδοντόπαστα	odhontopasta
toothpick	ὀδοντογλυφίδα	odhontoghlifidha
top	κορφή	korfi
torch	δαυλός	dhavlos
torn	σκισμένος	skismenos
touch (to)	ἀκουμπῶ	akoumbo
tourist	ἐπισκέπτης, τουρίστας	episkeptis, touristas
towards	πρός	pros
towel	πετσέτα	petseta
tower	πύργος	pirghos
town	πόλη	poli

toy	παιγνίδι	peghnidhi
traffic	κυκλοφορία	kikloforia
traffic jam	κυκλοφοριακός συνωστισμός	kikloforiakos sinostismos
traffic lights	κυκλοφοριακά φῶτα	kikloforiaka fota
train	τραῖνο	treno
translate (to)	μεταφράζω	metafrazo
travel (to)	ταξιδεύω	taxidhevo
travel agent	ταξιδιωτικό γραφεῖο	taxidhiotiko ghrafio
traveller	ταξιδιώτης	taxidhiotis
travellers' cheque	travellers' cheque	
treatment *manner*	τρόπος μεταχειρίσεως	tropos metakhirisseos
treatment *for illness*	θεραπεία	therapia
tree	δέντρο	dhentro
trip	ταξίδι	taxidhi
trouble	ἐνόχληση, ἀνησυχία, ταραχή	enohlissi, anissihia, tarahi
trousers	πανταλόνια	pantalonia
true	ἀληθινός	alithinos
trunk *luggage*	μπαοῦλο	baoulo
trunks	μαγιό	maghio
try, try on (to)	δοκιμάζω	dhokimazo
Tuesday	Τρίτη	triti

tunnel	σῆραγξ	siranx
turn (to)	γυρνῶ	ghirno
turning	γύρισμα, στροφή	ghirisma, strofi
twisted	στριμμένος	strimenos

U

ugly	ἄσκημος	askimos
umbrella	umbrella	
uncle	θεῖος	thios
uncomfortable	στενόχωρος	stenohoros
under	ἀπό κάτω	apo kato
underground	ὑπόγειος	ipoghios
understand	καταλαβαίνω	katalaveno
underwear	ἐσώρρουχα	essorouha
university	πανεπιστήμιο	panepistimio
unpack (to)	ξετυλίγω	ksetiligho
until	ἕως ὅτου, μέχρι	eos otou, mehri
unusual	ἀσυνήθης	assinithis
up	πάνω	pano
upstairs	ἐπάνω	epano
urgent	ἐπεῖγον	epighon
use (to)	χρησιμοποιῶ	hrissimopio
usual	συνήθης	sinithis

USA	Ἡνωμένες Πολιτεῖες Ἀμερικῆς—ΗΠΑ	inomenes polities amerikis
USSR	Ἡνωμένη Σοβιετική Σοσιαλιστική Δημοκρατία	inomeni sovietiki sossialistiki dhimokratia

V

vacant	ἐλεύθερος	eleftheros
vaccination	ἐμβολιασμός	emvoliasmos
valid	ἰσχύων	ishion
valley	κοιλάδα	kiladha
valuable	πολύτιμος	politimos
value	ἀξία	axia
vase	βάζο	vazo
vegetables	λαχανικά	lahanika
vegetarian	χορτοφάγος	hortofaghos
veil	βέλο	velo
vein	φλέβα	fleva
ventilation	ἐξαερισμός	exaerismos
very	πολύ	poli
very much	πάρα πολύ	para poli
vest	γελέκο	gheleko
view	θέα	thea
village	χωριό	horio

vinegar	ξύδι	xidhi
violin	βιολί	violi
visa	viza	
visit	ἐπίσκεψη	episkepsi
visit (to)	ἐπισκέπτομαι	episkeptome
voice	φωνή	foni
voltage	voltage	
vomit (to)	κάνω ἐμετό	kano emeto
voyage	ταξίδι	taxidhi

W

wait (to)	περιμένω	perimeno
waiter	σερβιτόρος	servitoros
waiting room	αἴθουσα ἀναμονῆς	ethoussa anamonis
waitress	σερβιτόρα	servitora
wake (to)	ξυπνῶ	ksipno
Wales	Οὐαλία	oualia
walk (to)	περπατῶ	perpato
wallet	πορτοφόλι	portofoli
want (to)	θέλω	thelo
wardrobe	γκαρνταρόμπα	gardaroba
warm	ζεστός	zestos
wash (to)	πλένω	pleno

washbasin	νιπτήρας	niptiras
watch	ρολόι	roloï
water	νερό	nero
waterfall	καταρράκτης	kataraktis
watermelon	καρπούζι	karpouzi
water ski-ing	θαλάσσιο σκί	thalassio ski
wave	κῦμα	kima
way	δρόμος	dhromos
we	ἐμεῖς	emis
wear (to)	φορῶ	foro
weather	καιρός	keros
Wednesday	Τετάρτη	tetarti
week	ἑβδομάδα	evdhomadha
weigh (to)	ζυγίζω	zighizo
well	καλά	kala
Welshman	Οὐαλός	oualos
west	δύση	dhissi
wet	βρεμμένος	vremenos
what ?	τί;	ti
wheel	τροχός, ρόδα	trohos, rodha
when ?	πότε;	pote
where ?	ποῦ;	pou
which ?	ποιό;	pio

while	κατά τή διάρκεια	kata ti dhiarkia
white	ἄσπρος	aspros
who?	ποιός;	pios
whole	ὁλόκληρος	olokliros
whose?	ποιοῦ, ποιανοῦ;	piou, pianou
why?	γιατί;	ghiati
wide	πλατύς, εὐρύς	platis, evris
widow	χήρα	hira
widower	χῆρος	hiros
wife	γυναίκα, σύζυγος	ghineka, sizighos
win (to)	κερδίζω	kerdhizo
wind	ἀέρας	aeras
window	παράθυρο	parathiro
wine	κρασί	krassi
wine list	λίστα κρασιῶν	lista krassion
winter	χειμώνας	himonas
wish (to)	θέλω	thelo
with	μέ	me (as in 'let')
without	χωρίς	horis
woman	γυναίκα	ghineka
wool	μαλλί	mali
word	λέξη	lexi
worse	χειρότερος	hiroteros

worth (to be)	ἀξίζω	axizo
wound	πληγή	plighi
wrap	τυλίγω	tiligho
wrist	καρπός χεριοῦ	karpos heriou
write (to)	γράφω	ghrafo
writing paper	χαρτί ἐπιστολογραφίας	harti epistologhrafias
wrong	λάθος	lathos

Y

yacht	yacht	
year	χρόνος	hronos
yellow	κίτρινος	kitrinos
yes	ναί	ne (as in 'let')
yesterday	χθές	hthes
you	ἐσύ	essi
young	νέος	neos
your, yours	σου, δικό σου	sou, dhiko sou
youth hostel	ξενώνας νέων	xenonas neon

Z

zip	φερμουάρ	fermouar
zoo	ζωολογικός κῆπος	zoologhikos kipos

503 drahmi to £1.00